Alberta
Seasonal
Cookbook

Jennifer Ogle
James Darcy

LONE PINE

Lone Pine Publishing

The Publisher: Lone Pine Publishing
10145–81 Avenue
Edmonton, AB, Canada T6E 1W9
Website: www.lonepinepublishing.com

Library and Archives Canada Cataloguing in Publication
Ogle, Jennifer, 1972-
   The Alberta seasonal cookbook / Jennifer Ogle, James Darcy.

Includes index.
ISBN–13: 978-1-55105-580-0
ISBN–10: 1-55105-580-5

   1. Cookery, Canadian—Alberta style. I. Title.

TX715.6.O4518 2007   641.597123   C2007-900027-4

Editorial Director: Nancy Foulds
Editorial: Carol Woo, Sandra Bit
Production Manager: Gene Longson
Book Design and Layout: Willa Kung, Elliot Engley
Cover Design: Gerry Dotto

Photography: All photographs by Nanette Samol, except p. 30, 48, 94, 140, 158, by Merle Prosofsky.
Food Stylist: Jennifer Ogle

Thank you to the following people who assisted with our photo shoots:
Alison Beck, Laura Peters, Lori Holowaychuk, Mary Lobay, Randy von Beiker

We acknowledge the financial support of the Government of Canada through the Book Publishing Industry Development Program (BPIDP) for our publishing activities.

PC: P14

CONTENTS

Introduction 4

Spring 8

Summer 43

Fall 86

Winter 120

Index 160

DEDICATION

For my brother, Matt Christopher Spring,
who happily eats anything I cook!

INTRODUCTION

Alberta is rich in locally grown, seasonally available products, including a diversity of meats, grains, fruit and vegetables. Artisanal cheese producers, microbreweries and specialty growers widen the variety even further. Alberta is the proud home of Taber corn, Mundare sausage, Innisfail lamb and Bles-Wold yogurt. Morels, chanterelles and other delicious mushrooms are available with a bit of knowledge and foraging. Trout and perch are among the fish native to Alberta.

Eating seasonally may seem an obvious idea, but how much do we really know about the food we eat every day? Where does it come from and how is it grown? What kind and how much fertilizer and pesticide remain on or in the product? Are the people who produce the food working with humane conditions and receiving adequate remuneration? Do we know the financial, ethical and environmental costs of transporting food around the world?

Locally grown foods, often organically grown, are fresher and tastier and support our local economy. Farmers' markets across the province showcase Alberta's bounty, from simple foods such as tomatoes, strawberries, eggplant and garden peas to bison jerky and kimchi. Half the fun in spending part of a Saturday at your local market comes from being able to actually speak to the producers, who are more than happy to explain how things are grown, give tips and even share family-tested recipes. Organic agriculture has grown some 20 percent a year over the past several years. Another source of locally grown products is your own back yard! Even if you have only a small plot of land or a balcony, you can grow many vegetables and fruits, and have plenty of fun doing it.

With this book, we have created a resource of recipes that represent the best of what Alberta has to offer. It makes sense to buy Alberta beef, but try braising it when chestnuts are available in the fall. Seville oranges come into season in late January and February; those short, cold days are the best time to make some marmalade for a special treat. Saskatoons are available in late summer; use them to make a pie to end a Labour Day barbecue. It's all here, in the appetizers, salads, soups, main dishes, sides, desserts and snacks that make up the seasons of this book.

About the Author

Canadian chef Jennifer Ogle learned her craft from a variety of sources, among them the renowned French cooking school *La Varenne,* which lead to an opportunity to work in the Michelin-starred restaurant *La Madeleine* in Burgundy, France.

Jennifer recalls that her love of cooking started at an early age, when many Sunday afternoons were spent experimenting in the kitchen. Today, Jennifer enjoys all aspects of the culinary world, from cooking to writing, with a particular passion for seasonal, local ingredients.

In Our Kitchen

We have found the following ingredient choices and cooking procedures to be successful in our kitchen and recommend them highly wherever possible.

Butter is unsalted and is easiest to measure using the convenient markings on the wrapping.

Citrus juices are fresh squeezed.

Eggs are large, free-run eggs. They should be at room temperature for baking.

Flour is unbleached all-purpose.

Herbs are fresh, unless stated otherwise. In a pinch, the best alternative to fresh is frozen, not dried. You can freeze herbs yourself in the summer when they are plentiful, and you can even find them in the freezer section of some of the better grocery stores.

Mushrooms, such as morels and chanterelles, can be found in the wild, but we advise that you confirm the identification of mushrooms with an experienced collector before cooking them; some species of mushrooms are acutely toxic and can cause death.

Stocks are homemade. Good quality stocks available in tetra packs are the best substitute. Avoid using those nasty little cubes. Miso, a fermented soybean paste, is another interesting alternative to stock, and it will keep in the refrigerator for several months. Stir it in 1 Tbsp (15 mL) at a time until you have a rich, full flavour.

Sugar is organic and unrefined rather than white and bleached. When looking for a rich brown sugar, use muscovado sugar, available in grocery and health food stores. It still contains the minerals and vitamins originally in the sugar cane plant, and it has a full molasses flavour.

Yeast is regular dry yeast; 1/2 oz (15 g) dry yeast is equal to 1 Tbsp fresh yeast.

Essential Ingredients

The following ingredients are used in many of the recipes in this book; special ingredients found in just one or two recipes are described where they are used. Some items are widely available, whereas others are best sought in gourmet, specialty food, health food or ethnic stores or obtained by mail order or the Internet.

Bay Leaves— Fresh leaves have such a different flavour that they are worth the effort to find. They are occasionally available at large grocery stores and can be specially ordered. In a well-sealed container in the fridge, they can last three or four months.

Coconut Milk—Use unsweetened coconut milk in cans. Naturally sweet, it is often better than cream in savory dishes.

Garlic—Use fresh garlic! An Italian friend once told me that if you can't be bothered to peel and chop fresh garlic you shouldn't be allowed to use it!

Lemons and Limes—Use fresh! You can't compare the taste to concentrate.

Mayonnaise—It's always better homemade:

5 egg yolks

$2/3$ cup (150 mL) extra virgin olive oil

$1/4$ cup (60 mL) good quality vinegar or juice of 1 lemon

pinch of sea salt to taste

- You need both hands free to make mayonnaise. Spread a damp cloth on your counter, nestle a medium-sized bowl in its centre and wrap it around base of bowl to keep it steady while you whisk.

- Whisk yolk, vinegar and salt in bowl until well combined and yolk has lightened in colour.

- Add oil, a drop at a time, whisking continuously until mixture emulsifies and thickens.

- When about half of oil has been added, add remaining oil in a slow, steady stream. Store, covered, in refrigerator for up to 5 days. You can thin your mayonnaise by lightly whisking in some water.

- Many people like to add mustard or fresh herbs to their mayonnaise. Adding minced garlic turns plain mayonnaise into aioli. Makes just over 1 cup (250 mL).

Mustard—Use good quality mustard for everything from sandwiches to dressings to sauces. When you are down to the last few teaspoons clinging to the bottom of your mustard jar, add fresh lemon juice, olive oil, sea salt and fresh pepper for a yummy impromptu salad dressing. Just shake and enjoy.

Oil, Sesame—Use for a nutty flavour addition. Store it in the fridge.

Oil, Olive—Extra virgin olive oil is indispensable. Try olive oil from Italy, Spain or Greece.

Oil, Grape Seed —Use for higher heat cooking.

Pepper, Fresh—Please don't use pre-ground pepper; it has such poor flavour. A variety of peppercorns are available. Black or white can be used interchangeably in any of the recipes.

Salt—Great salt is the key to great cooking. Salt brings out the flavour in food. Sea salt, kosher salt, Celtic salt—choose a favourite. Better yet, obtain some of each. Using a better quality salt also means that you will use less, because the flavour is more intense. If you need to reduce salt even further for health reasons, use fresh herbs, various spices and flavour lifters, such as lemon juice, to maintain the flavour intensity while reducing the salt content.

Soy Sauce—Both tamari and shoyu are high quality, fermented and chemical-free "soy sauces" that are used to enhance flavour and impart a unique saltiness.

Star Anise—This strongly anise-scented Oriental spice is commonly sold dried, as quarter-sized, star-shaped clusters of 5 to 10 pods, each containing a single seed. The seeds can be used on their own, crushed or ground, or the entire stars can be added, then removed.

Vinegar, Apple Cider—Use when you need an all-purpose vinegar; organic, unrefined and unpasteurized has the best flavour.

Vinegar, Balsamic—Its unique flavour is great in everything from soups to sweets. Be sure to try authentic balsamic from Modena, Italy.

Measuring

Dry ingredients should be spooned into the measuring cup and leveled off with a knife or spatula.

Measurements are in both metric and imperial. Note that for butter, a pound is considered to be 454 g; for meat, vegetables, etc., a pound is 500 g.

Solids, including butter and most cheeses, are measured in dry-measure cups and liquids in liquid-measure cups.

Spring Heirloom Tomato Salad

Serves 4

If you are interested in tomatoes—those tomatoes reminiscent of days in the garden as a child picking the sun-warmed fruit right off the vine—then look no further than Hotchkiss tomatoes. Grown on a Calgary area family-owned farm dedicated to growing heirloom tomatoes, over 30 varieties of Hotchkiss can be found at high-end restaurants and specialty markets across the province. Tomatoes (Solanum lycopersicum) are native to the Americas and were brought to Europe in the 16th century. Although the Europeans admired tomatoes for their beauty, they initially believed the entire plant to be poisonous. The leaves and stems do indeed contain toxic compounds, but the fruits are quite edible. Other sources say the reason for the tomato's slow acceptance at European dinner tables was because the lead in pewter plates reacted with the fruit, causing it to leach into the tomatoes.

1 clove garlic, minced

splash of white balsamic vinegar (see Essential Ingredients, p. 6)

¼ cup (60 mL) olive oil

sea salt and freshly ground pepper to taste

1 lb (500 g) heirloom tomatoes, washed, cored and sliced ½ in (1 cm) thick

½ lb (250 g) bocconcini, sliced the same thickness as the tomatoes

handful of fresh basil leaves, washed and patted dry

French baguette

In a salad bowl, add the garlic, vinegar and oil. Then add the tomatoes, tossing gently to coat with dressing. Season to taste with salt and pepper.

On individual plates, layer tomato slices with bocconcini and some basil tucked in between and around the tomato slices. Scatter remaining basil leaves on top and drizzle remaining dressing.

Serve with slices of crusty French baguette.

Tip
Fresh tomatoes from the garden or the farmers' market would also work in this recipe.

Bocconcini is a semi-ripe mozzarella cheese that comes in small, soft, white balls.

In her tomato book, the late Lois Hole, beloved lieutenant-governor of Alberta and long-time gardening guru, wrote about the importance of heirloom varieties in maintaining gene pool diversity. Lois called this contribution priceless because the heirloom seeds are used in developing new varieties that have natural resistance to viral, fungal and bacterial diseases.

Asparagus and Chèvre Salad

Serves 4

Alberta, like other Canadian provinces, is dotted with artisan goat cheese producers. Natricia Dairy, located in the heart of Alberta *and* the heart of Alberta's dairy land, is the province's largest producer of goat cheese. *Chèvre* is the French word for "goat," and it has become synonymous with the French-style, tangy, fluffy, soft cheese made from goat's milk. Most grocery-store varieties are mild, moist and creamy and come in logs or cylinders, sometimes rolled in herbs or spices such as peppercorns, or coated with ash or edible leaves. Goat's milk can also be made into other types of cheese, including feta, Gouda and Brie. As well, chèvre can be fashioned into other shapes, such as pyramids. Somewhat more piquant in taste than cheeses made with cow's milk, chèvre is often more easily digested by people with lactose intolerance; it also has twice the protein and one-third the calories.

1 bunch (about 2 lb [1 kg]) asparagus, trimmed

splash of olive oil

sea salt and freshly ground pepper to taste

1 lb (500 g) package frozen peas, refreshed in boiling water, drained and cooled

1 cup (250 g) chèvre, crumbled

½ cup (125 mL) fresh mint, chopped

½ cup (125 mL) fresh basil, chopped

1 lime cut into 4 wedges

Preheat barbecue to medium-high heat. Toss trimmed asparagus with olive oil, salt and pepper. Grill for 4 minutes, turning once. Set aside.

In a bowl, toss together the remaining ingredients, except the lime. Cut the warm asparagus into bite-sized pieces and add to the bowl, toss and season again if needed. (You cut the asparagus after because it is much easier to grill if left whole!) Divide among 4 plates and garnish each salad with a lime wedge.

Tip
Soft cheeses such as chèvre do not slice well, often ending up as a crumbled mess that sticks to the knife. The easiest way to cut a soft cheese is with a piece of taut dental floss—just be sure to use unflavoured!

Tip
Allow cheese to come to room temperature for at least 30 minutes (longer for hard cheese or if the room is particularly cold) before serving in order to enjoy its full flavour and aroma. Portion cheese, if desired, while cold and keep it wrapped so it doesn't dry out before you are ready to serve.

Lobster Cocktail

Serves 6

"Surf 'n turf," also known as steak and lobster, became a popular menu item in steakhouses across Alberta in the boom years of the 1970s. Surf 'n turf has evolved to include any combo of seafood and meat, but the pairing of Alberta's favourite red meat and the succulent lobster remains a fixture on menus throughout the province. Spring marks the start of lobster season in Atlantic Canada, and spring lobsters are regarded as the best quality because of their thick shells, high meat content and excellent taste. The Alberta Acadian Society, founded in 1986, brings together Acadian Albertans for social and cultural gatherings. An event worth noting is the annual Lobster Supper, which is held in late May or early June.

1 x 8 oz (250 g) lobster, fresh or frozen (thawed and squeezed of excess liquid)

3 Tbsp (45 mL) mayonnaise

1 tsp (5 mL) mustard

1 Tbsp (15 mL) fresh mint, chopped

1 Tbsp (15 mL) fresh tarragon, chopped

½ tsp (2 mL) lime zest

½ tsp (2 mL) orange zest

juice of ½ lime

1 tsp (5 mL) horseradish, or more to taste

1 Tbsp (15 mL) capers, squeezed dry and chopped

⅓ cup (75 mL) roasted red bell pepper, diced small

sea salt and freshly ground pepper to taste

Mix lobster, mayonnaise and the rest of ingredients, except for avocado and season with salt and pepper. In a separate bowl, toss avocado cubes in lime juice. To serve, layer the lobster with the avocado. Garnish with green onions or caviar and serve as an appetizer with your favourite crackers. Makes approximately 3 cups (750 mL).

Spicy horseradish (Armoracia rusticana) *is the root of a perennial herb native to Europe and Asia—the aroma alone is enough to make a grown man cry.*

Now naturalized in North America, horseradish can be very difficult to eradicate once planted in your garden. It grows wild in Alberta, and starting in late spring, is available at local farmers' markets. It adds zip to this lobster cocktail.

Avocado Mix
1 avocado, peeled and cubed into small dice
juice of ½ lime

Garnish
green onions, sliced or caviar

Cipollini and Asiago Stuffed Morels

Serves 4 as an appetizer

Alberta is the proud home of the only mycological club in Canada's prairie provinces, the Edmonton Mycological Society. The organization holds an annual morel forage in May, with forays throughout the year in the Rocky Mountain foothills, northern Aspen Parkland and southern Boreal Forest ecozones of Alberta. Highly prized for their meaty, mushroomy flavour, morels (*Morchella*) are edible cup fungi. Morels generally grow year after year on the same forested sites, preferring the company of ash trees, but they flourish in the years immediately following a forest fire. Another mushroom worth mentioning is Alberta's official mushroom (as of 2006), the red cap mushroom (*Leccinum boreale*).

1 Tbsp (15 mL) grape seed or canola oil

½ cup (125 mL) cipollini onion, peeled and quartered

1 lb (500 g) fresh morels, reserve 12 of the largest ones, left whole, the rest chopped for stuffing

¼ cup (60 mL) white wine

1 clove garlic, minced

¼ cup (60 mL) parsley, chopped

2 Tbsp (30 mL) chives, chopped

¼ cup (60 mL) grated Asiago cheese

2 to 3 Tbsp (30 to 45 mL) panko

sea salt and pepper to taste

In a medium saucepan, heat the oil over medium heat and sauté the cipollini onion until they start to caramelize, about 5 minutes. Add the chopped mushrooms, white wine and cook for about 5 minutes. Add garlic, cook for 2 to 3 minutes and remove pan from heat. Stir in remaining ingredients, except for the 12 reserved morels. Stuff them with the filling.

For the lime mayonnaise, stir together lime zest and mayonnaise. Set aside.

For breading, place flour, eggs and panko into separate bowls. Heat clarified butter in a saucepan over medium-high heat. Bread the stuffed morels one at a time, dipping first in the flour, then the egg and finally the panko. Cook the mushrooms in the butter until brown and crispy. Serve hot with lime mayonnaise.

Tip
To remove any unwanted critters hiding in the morels, soak mushrooms in salted water for at least one hour.

Tip
To make clarified butter, melt unsalted butter slowly over low heat. Gradually, froth will rise to the top with a layer of clear golden oil in the middle and a layer of milk solids on the bottom. Clarified butter is the middle layer. Skim off the froth and carefully ladle out the clear oil, leaving out the milk solids.

Lime mayonnaise

zest from 1 lime

½ cup (125 mL) mayonnaise (see
Essential Ingredients, p. 6)

Breading

½ cup (125 mL) flour

3 eggs, lightly beaten

2 cups (500 mL) panko

1 cup (250 mL) clarified butter

Panko is a coarser variety of breadcrumbs, which has a crispier texture when fried. It can be found in Asian markets.

If you can't find fresh morels, frozen ones will work well too.

Cream of Asparagus Soup

Serves 6

With a short season extending from May to the end of June, fresh asparagus (*Asparagus officinalis*) offers a much-anticipated break from the winter blues. Asparagus is a member of the lily family. The name most likely comes from either the Persian word *asparag*, meaning sprout, or from the Greek word ασπηαραγοσ, meaning "long as one's throat." It grows well in Alberta's cooler climate, and it is even said that plants can survive for decades on the Prairies in a cultivated field or as a roadside weed. Edgar Farm, located in Innisfail, has the largest field of asparagus in the province, a full 17 acres (7 hectares) of it. The Edgars have discovered that by sacrificing some yield and using the cool weather to their advantage, they can produce a delicious, sweeter-than-normal asparagus. Check out farmers' markets and U-pick gardens for fresh asparagus starting in May.

2 Tbsp (30 mL) unsalted butter

2 Tbsp (30 mL) olive oil

1 large yellow onion, diced

¼ cup (60 mL) white wine

2 sweet potatoes, diced

½ tsp fresh thyme, chopped

¼ cup (60 mL) parsley, chopped

2 stalks celery, diced

2 cloves garlic, minced

sea salt to taste

8 cups (2 L) chicken or vegetable stock

1 cup (250 mL) heavy cream (32%)

2 lbs (1 kg) fresh asparagus, roughly chopped, reserve some tips for garnish

1 cup (250 mL) packed fresh spinach

fresh lemon juice

Garnish

¼ cup (60 mL) heavy cream (32%)

pinch of sea salt

fresh lemon juice

In a medium pot, heat butter and oil. Add onions and sauté until golden. Add white wine and bring to a rapid boil on high heat until liquid is reduced, about 3 to 5 minutes. Add sweet potatoes, thyme, parsley, celery, garlic, salt and stock and bring to a boil. Immediately reduce heat to a simmer and cook until sweet potatoes are soft, about 15 minutes.

Add cream, asparagus and spinach, and bring to a gentle simmer. When the asparagus are tender, about 5 minutes, remove from heat and purée in a blender until smooth. Season with a good squeeze of fresh lemon juice. Taste and adjust seasoning. Serve hot in bowls with a garnish of heavy cream seasoned with a pinch of salt and a splash of fresh lemon juice on top.

Tip
By snapping off the lower ends of the asparagus, you ensure that you are getting the most tender part of the spear. Alternatively, you can use a vegetable peeler: start about two-thirds from the bottom end and peel the more fibrous outer layer, exposing the tender flesh.

Tip
Store asparagus upright in about an inch (2 to 3 cm) of water and keep them refrigerated because the sugars can turn to starch quickly.

Variation
White asparagus tastes the same as green asparagus and can be used in the same ways. Rarer and thus more expensive, it is grown by keeping the tender shoots covered with soil and away from sunlight.

Spring Lamb Tagine with Preserved Lemons and Olives

Serves 6

Sheep farming had a tumultuous start here, which may explain why lamb is not as popular today as beef and chicken. By 1884 the battle between cattle ranchers and sheep farmers had grown bitter and the federal government, in support of the cattlemen, banned sheep in southwestern Alberta from the U.S. border north to the Bow River. Today, lamb is becoming more and more popular, and Canadians are being drawn to Alberta lamb—in fact, Innisfail lamb makes it onto the menus of the great restaurants of the country. The defining factor in your decision to buy Alberta lamb should be the flavour: because it is fed grain, not grass, it is uniquely mild compared to lamb grown elsewhere in the world. It is believed that sheep were domesticated by 8900 BC, in the area that is now Iraq and Romania. Of course, some of the oldest recipes for lamb come from Greece, where lamb is still a favourite.

olive oil, about ¼ cup (60 mL)

1½ lbs (750 g) lamb shoulder meat, cubed

1 yellow onion, diced

2 cups (500 mL) lamb stock (see next page)

2 large ripe tomatoes, chopped

1 small turnip, peeled and cubed

2 carrots, peeled and sliced

½ preserved lemon (p. 154), finely chopped

2 cups (500 mL) Cerignola olives, or other unpitted green olives

⅓ cup (75 mL) dried apricots, sliced

1 bunch cilantro, chopped, some reserved for garnish

¼ cup (60 mL) parsley, chopped

1 clove garlic, minced

1 tsp (5 mL) cinnamon

1 tsp (5 mL) coriander

harissa to taste

sea salt and freshly ground pepper to taste

Preheat oven to 325° F (160° C). Heat a splash of olive oil in a large ovenproof pot and brown the lamb in small batches, adding more oil, if necessary. Add onion and sauté for 5 minutes. Combine remaining ingredients and bring to a boil. Cover and bake in oven for about 2 hours until meat is tender. Serve with couscous.

Couscous

Heat stock or water with oil in a small saucepan to a gentle boil. Stir in couscous. Remove from heat and leave it covered for 5 minutes. Fluff with a fork before serving. Makes about 3 cups.

Lamb Stock

Cover lamb bones with cold water and bring to a boil. Reduce to a simmer and skim off the froth as it rises to the surface. Add the rest of ingredients and simmer for about 2 hours. Strain through a fine sieve and cool. Refrigerate overnight and remove the layer of fat.

Stock will keep for 4 days refrigerated or 2 months frozen. Makes about 5 cups.

Couscous

1¼ cups (310 mL) stock or water

1 Tbsp canola oil

1¼ cups (310 mL) couscous

Lamb Stock

1 lb (500 g) lamb bones

8 cups water

1 yellow onion, peeled and sliced in half

1 carrot, peeled and cut in chunks

1 parsnip, peeled and cut in chunks

½ cup (125 mL) celery, cut in chunks

1 tsp (5 mL) black peppercorns

1 clove garlic

Broccoli and Tempeh Rice Bowl

Serves 4

In Alberta, fresh local broccoli becomes available in June and, weather permitting, can last through the first two weeks of October. A member of the cabbage family, broccoli *(Brassica oleracea)* is a very close relative of cauliflower. Not that long ago in Alberta, broccoli was an unfamiliar vegetable favoured by the province's Italian immigrants. (In fact, it was eaten in what is now Tuscany long before it was eaten anywhere else, and it was adopted by the Romans when they invaded the region.) When it first came to Great Britain, broccoli was known as "Italian asparagus." Nowadays, broccoli makes the grade as a popular super-food, because it is loaded with vitamins and the anti-cancer enzyme sulforaphane. "Canadian broccoli," otherwise known as "Russian Red," although a member of the same family of vegetables, is not broccoli at all, but a type of kale.

2 Tbsp (30 mL) soy sauce

1 Tbsp (30 mL) mirin or sweet rice wine

2 Tbsp (30 mL) light miso

1 tsp (5 mL) toasted sesame oil

¼ tsp (1 mL) cornstarch

2 tsp (10 mL) grape seed or canola oil

1 Tbsp (15 mL) ginger, finely chopped

2 tsp (10 mL) lemongrass, tender bottom part only, chopped

2 garlic cloves, minced

1 package Indonesian-style tempeh, cut into ½-inch strips

1 head of broccoli, cut into florets

½ cup (125 mL) each yellow and red pepper, cut into strips

½ cup (125 mL) snow peas

½ cup (125 mL) green onions, cut in ¼-inch diagonal strips

2 tsp (10 mL) black sesame seeds

½ tsp (2 mL) sea salt

2 cups (500 mL) hot, cooked brown rice

In a small bowl, combine soy sauce, mirin, miso, sesame oil, and cornstarch, stirring with a whisk and set aside. Heat oil in a large skillet over medium-high heat and sauté ginger, lemongrass and garlic for 1 minute or just until mixture begins to brown. Add tempeh and sauté for 2 minutes, then add broccoli, peppers, snow peas and sauté for 1 minute. Add to skillet and cook for 1 minute, until sauce has slightly thickened. Remove from heat and stir in green onions, sesame seeds and salt. Serve over rice.

Tip
Soak your broccoli in warm, salted water to get rid of any critters. As with all members of the cabbage family, broccoli is best used within a few days of picking to retain its sweet flavour and mild odour.

Tempeh is a fermented soybean product that has been enjoyed in Southeast Asia for centuries. It is fermented with a *Rhizopus* mould, which makes the soy protein more easily digestible. Tempeh has a deep, nutty flavour and can be used in meals as a substitute for tofu or meat. Here in Alberta, it is available at most supermarkets.

Gnocchi in a Sorrel Sauce

Serves 2 as a main course, 4 as a side dish

Sorrel *(Rumex acetosa)* is a perennial herb with a sharp, thirst-quenching lemony flavour. Not yet wildly popular in Alberta, sorrel is perfectly suited to our climate, is frost tolerant and is an excellent addition to anyone's garden. Sorrel comes up early in spring and can be enjoyed through to autumn. To keep leaves tender and mild, pinch off flowers as they come up. Sorrel is found growing wild throughout the province; it is available at local farmers' markets, and it occasionally turns up in the herb section of large grocery stores. Sorrel can be used in anything from soups to salads and stews, and it can be puréed and frozen for winter use. It is a staple in the cuisine of central Europe, where it is cultivated as a vegetable. Sorrel most often appears in a type of soup enriched with egg and sour cream, which is believed to share the same culinary history as borscht.

1 lb (500 g) package gnocchi
splash olive oil
1 Tbsp (15 mL) unsalted butter
1 small shallot, minced
½ cup (125 mL) white wine
1 cup (250 mL) heavy cream (32%)
1 packed cup (250 g) sorrel, chopped
¼ cup (60 mL) parsley, chopped
sea salt and freshly ground pepper to taste
good sized pinch of fresh chives, chopped
handful fresh grated Parmesan cheese

Bring a big pot of salted water to a rolling boil and cook the gnocchi until they float to the surface. Drain, toss with a splash of olive oil and set aside.

In a large saucepan, heat the butter and add the shallot and cook for 2 to 3 minutes, then add the white wine and cook until the wine has reduced by half. Add the cream and continue cooking for 5 minutes at medium-high heat.

Purée sorrel and parsley in a blender along with hot cream mixture until everything is incorporated; the sauce turns a jade green colour. Pour sauce back into pan along with the gnocchi just to heat through and season with salt and pepper. Serve in warm bowls with chives and Parmesan cheese sprinkled on top.

"Gnocchi" is Italian for "dumplings"; the singular, "gnocco," means "lump." Gnocchi are often made using potatoes, but they can also be made with durum wheat, flour or ricotta cheese. Traditionally, gnocchi are served with tomato sauce or melted butter and Parmesan cheese, but they lend themselves well to almost any sauce.

Herb Pesto

Makes about 2 cups (500 mL)

Basil *(Ocimum basilicum)* thrives in the heat of summer, and it will grow in abundance if it is kept in a humid environment. It does not tolerate cold weather, so when growing basil in Alberta, be sure there is no chance of frost. It can also be planted indoors, preferably in a south-facing window. Basil is thought to have originated in India, where it was considered a holy plant and often planted near shrines and temples. Legend has it that the Greeks named the plant βασιλευς, meaning "king," when it was found growing above the spot where the Holy Cross was rediscovered in the 4th century AD. Even today, basil is considered the high priest of herbs. There are dozens of varieties available, from licorice basil and cinnamon-flavoured basil to purple varieties and spicy warm ones, such as Thai basil.

4 cups (32 oz) fresh basil leaves, rinsed, patted dry and well packed

4 cloves garlic, peeled

1 cup (250 mL) pine nuts or other nut of your choice

1½ cups (375 mL) freshly grated Parmesan or Pecorino cheese

1½ cups (375 mL) extra virgin olive oil

sea salt and freshly ground pepper to taste

In a blender, pulse basil and garlic until well crushed. Add nuts, process to crush, then add cheese. You should have a thick paste. Slowly drizzle in olive oil, continuously mixing. Adjust seasoning and serve with pasta or vegetables, or add to a soup, etc.

Tip
Traditionally, pesto is made in a mortar and pestle. A food processor also works just fine—the method is the same.

Variation
Genoa, Italy, is the birthplace of pesto, where it is traditionally made with basil and pine nuts. For variety, try other herbs, such as arugula, cilantro or even cooked artichokes, or nuts and seeds, such as walnuts and sunflower kernels.

Potato Frittata

Serves 4

Potatoes have always formed part of the backbone of the diet of Albertans. Cheap, easy to cook and tasty, they are a comfort food and adapt well in many recipes. Alberta has close to 52,000 acres (21,000 hectares) of land dedicated to potato growing, which translates into 9 billion spuds every year. Alberta is the third largest grower in the country, after Prince Edward Island and Manitoba. The average Canadian eats about 163 pounds (74 kilograms) of potatoes per year! From the Italian word *fritto* ("fried"), a frittata is an open-faced omelette made with cheese and other ingredients mixed into the eggs. It is a classic Roman dish traditionally served on Easter Day. Incorporating potatoes into this breakfast dish makes it an especially satisfying and comforting one-dish meal.

2 Tbsp (30 mL) butter

3 onions, sliced

2 medium Yukon Gold potatoes, peeled. cooked and sliced

8 eggs

¾ cup (175 mL) cream or milk

sea salt and freshly ground black pepper

½ cup (125 mL) aged Cheddar cheese, grated

1 Tbsp (15 mL) fresh thyme, chopped

Preheat broiler to 500° F (260° C). Melt butter in a 9-inch nonstick, ovenproof pan over low heat. Add onions and sauté, stirring occasionally, for 10 to 15 minutes until onions are golden brown. Add potato slices and cook until starting to brown, about 5 minutes. Whisk eggs, cream or milk, salt and pepper in a bowl to combine. Pour egg mixture over onions in frying pan and sprinkle with cheese and thyme. Cook frittata for 5 to 6 minutes or until it is almost set. To finish cooking, place frittata under broiler for 1 minute. Cut into wedges and serve along with your breakfast favourites.

The Yukon Gold potato, now the favourite of chefs around the world for its texture, flavour and tempting golden flesh, was bred by Canadian Gary Johnston and his colleagues at the University of Guelph in the 1960s.

Braised Swiss Chard

Serves 4

This cool-climate vegetable is an ideal Alberta vegetable, as it can withstand frost, and when planted in early spring, it is usually ready to eat within four to six weeks. It also rivals spinach as a great leafy green because, unlike spinach, it contains no oxalic acid, allowing the minerals it contains to be more readily digestible. Chard *(Beta vulgaris* var. *cicla;* sometimes known as silverbeet) is a kind of beet grown for its leaves rather than its roots. Chard packs a huge amount of vitamin A and is naturally high in sodium—one cup (250 ml) contains 313 mg. It is indigenous to the Mediterranean, but it is called Swiss chard as a result of its initial scientific description in the 16th century by a Swiss botanist.

2 small red onions, chopped

1 Tbsp (15 mL) butter

2 lbs (1 kg) chard leaves, stems removed

¼ cup (60 mL) white wine

sea salt and freshly ground pepper to taste

Sauté the onions in the butter over medium heat in a large pan until they are nearly softened and lightly browned, about 8 to 10 minutes. Meanwhile, clean chard leaves (see Tip) and slice into ribbons.

Add the chard leaves and wine. Cook rapidly, stirring frequently, until the chard is wilted and the liquid has evaporated, about 5 minutes.

Season with salt and pepper, and serve as a side dish.

Tip
To clean chard, simply swish in cool water and pat dry. The stems and leaves are both edible, but should be cooked separately because the stems take longer to cook.

Chard can be used instead of spinach or kale in your favourite recipes.

Pan-fried Fiddlehead Greens

Serves 4 to 6

Ostrich fern *(Matteuccia struthiopteris)* grows across the country in moist or wet forested areas, but the consumption of fiddleheads is most strongly associated with New Brunswick; up to 23,000 kilograms are gathered there annually. Long harvested by the Mi'kmaq and Maliseet peoples of eastern Canada, this seasonal treat is appreciated equally for the joy of the harvest as for the taste. These First Nations people were, and still are, crazy about this little fern, which they consider a delicacy. They believe it has a cleansing quality, a sort of rejuvenation after the long winter months. Even today, it is referred to as the first fruit of the season, the first of nature's offerings to peek through the soil after the long, cold winter. Luckily, given that the wild harvest is only a short three weeks and the best growing spots are carefully guarded family secrets, we can find fiddleheads in some grocery stores—including several brands of frozen ones—and at local farmers' markets. Watch your sources carefully in spring for this unusual fern to make its appearance.

1 lb (500 g) fresh fiddleheads

⅓ cup (75 mL) unsalted butter

juice of ½ lemon

pinch each of sea salt, pepper, paprika

⅓ cup (75 mL) fine breadcrumbs

Clean fiddleheads well and cook in boiling, salted water for 5 to 7 minutes. In a pan, melt butter and add lemon juice, salt, pepper, paprika and breadcrumbs. Toss hot fiddleheads in pan to coat well. Serves 6 as a side dish.

Tip
A great way to clean the papery, brown scales from fiddleheads is to shake them in small batches in a paper bag.

Traditional Steamed Fiddlehead Greens
Prepare fiddleheads by washing them well in several changes of clean water, then steam until tender, about 10 minutes. While still hot, toss with butter and vinegar. Season with salt and pepper.

1 lb (500 g) fresh fiddleheads

¼ cup (60 mL) unsalted butter

2 Tbsp (30 mL) champagne vinegar or cider vinegar

sea salt and pepper to taste

Hot Cross Buns

Makes 12

For many Albertans, Easter wouldn't be the same without spicy, sweet hot cross buns. Eaten in many Christian countries on Good Friday, hot cross buns are adorned with a cross (often made of pastry or icing) that symbolizes the crucifixion of Christ. The origins of the bun are likely a mixture of Christian and pagan traditions. One story is that during the Lenten season, Queen Elizabeth I of England attempted to ban the buns along with Roman Catholicism. When it became evident that the practice of putting a cross on buns could not be stopped, she passed a law that limited consumption of the buns to certain religious ceremonies. Supporters of hot cross buns at the time claimed that the buns would not rise without the cross, leading some culinary historians to believe that the first hot cross buns were scored with a knife, rather than decorated with pastry. Whatever their origin, hot cross buns are a welcome treat after the long Lenten fast.

1 Tbsp (15 mL) quick-rise yeast

¼ cup (60 mL) sugar

¼ cup (60 mL) warm water

2 cups (500 mL) unbleached bread flour

⅓ cup (75 mL) stone-ground whole grain bread flour

1 tsp (5 mL) sea salt

½ tsp (2 mL) each dried cinnamon, coriander and lavender

½ tsp (2 mL) freshly grated nutmeg

2 Tbsp (30 mL) cold unsalted butter, diced

⅓ cup (75 mL) currants

¼ cup (60 mL) golden raisins

¼ cup (60 mL) mixed fruit peel, finely chopped

1 large egg, beaten

1 cup (250 ml) milk

Prepare 1 parchment-lined baking sheet.

Put the yeast and 1 Tbsp of sugar in a small bowl with warm water until dissolved. Let sit 10 minutes.

Combine the flours, salt and spices in a bowl. Add the diced butter and rub into the flour using the tips of your fingers until the mixture looks like fine crumbs. Mix in currants, golden raisins and mixed fruit peel, then make a well in the centre of the mixture.

Add the yeast mixture, the remaining sugar and beaten egg to the well and approximately half the milk. Gradually add enough milk to the flour-fruit mixture to make a soft, but not sticky, dough. Add more milk, if necessary, or extra flour, if the dough is too sticky.

Turn the dough onto a lightly floured work surface and knead thoroughly for 10 minutes.

Return the dough to the bowl and then cover the bowl with plastic wrap. Let rise in a warm spot in the kitchen until doubled in size, about 1½ hours.

Punch down the dough a couple of times to deflate and divide it into 12 equal pieces. Shape each into a neat ball and set well apart on the baking sheet. Slip the baking sheet into large plastic bags and let rise as before until doubled in size, 45 minutes to 1 hour.

Meanwhile, preheat the oven to 400°F (200°C).

To make the dough for the cross pattern, put flour, butter and sugar into a small bowl and rub butter into the flour with the tips of your fingers until the mixture looks like coarse crumbs. Stir in cold water and mix; the dough will be firm. Roll the pastry into a long, thin rope about ⅛ inch (3mm) thick and cut into segments approximately 3 inches (8 cm) long.

When the buns are ready, uncover and brush with a little water to dampen, then place the cross pattern on top of the buns. Bake for 15 to 20 minutes until golden brown.

Meanwhile, to prepare the glaze, combine honey and milk until smooth. As soon as the buns are done, place them on a cooling rack and brush immediately with the hot glaze. Eat warm or toasted, or freeze for up to 1 month.

Pastry cross

⅓ cup (75 mL) white flour

scant ¼ cup (60 mL) cold unsalted butter, diced

2 tsp (10 mL) sugar

1 to 2 Tbsp (15 to 30 mL) cold water

Glaze

3 Tbsp (45 mL) honey

3 Tbsp (45 mL) milk

Asparagus Omelette

Serves 1

Eggs have long been associated with spring, rebirth and immortality. In many cultures, Easter eggs are elaborately decorated and given as gifts, the most extravagant being the Fabergé eggs of the Russian tsars. Perhaps the most famous decorated eggs are the pysanka. These eggs, decorated using the written-wax batik method that dates back to the Trypillian culture, continue to be hugely popular in many central and eastern European countries. In Ukraine, it is believed that the fate of the world rests on the continuation of the pysanka tradition. In Vegreville, this belief has been taken very seriously: in 1974 the town erected the world's largest pysanka, which is surely the most popular of all the BIG Alberta roadside attractions. As far as edible eggs are concerned, Alberta produces more than 45,000 dozen eggs per year, with a growing percentage of them being organic and free-range. These "designer eggs" are in such high demand in Alberta that they need to be supplemented with eggs from other provinces.

3 eggs, separated

2 Tbsp (30 mL) cream
(10 to 18 %)

1 Tbsp (15 mL) unsalted
butter

pinch sea salt and freshly
ground pepper

6 thin asparagus stalks, or
3 thick, lightly steamed

2 Tbsp (30 mL) Boursin
cheese, herb and garlic
or pepper

1 Tbsp (15 mL) fresh
chopped chives

In a medium bowl, blend egg yolks and cream with a fork. In another bowl, beat the whites until soft peaks form. Gently fold the whites into the yolks. In a nonstick 10-inch (25 cm) pan, melt butter over medium-high heat. Pour in eggs, swirling around pan to distribute evenly. Season with salt and pepper. Using a spatula, push the eggs gently around to allow the uncooked egg to flow underneath, run the spatula around the sides of the omelette to loosen. When it is almost set, about 40 seconds, lay the asparagus and cheese in the middle of the omelette. Fold one-third of the omelette over the filling, then lift the pan and slide the opposite third onto your plate and fold the omelette onto itself, forming a neat tri-fold package. Sprinkle with chives and serve immediately.

Tip
When buying asparagus, choose firm, bright green stalks for the best flavour.

Asparagus is an excellent source of folic acid, vitamin C and antioxidants.

Maple Syrup Pie

Serves 6

Even though Alberta doesn't consume maple syrup in the same quantities as Quebec, the sweet and distinctive treat is synonymous with both spring and Canada. First Nations peoples were the first to harvest the sap of maple trees. Each year, they set up sugar camps in the mid-altitude maple groves of northeastern North America and used buckets made from birch to collect the sap. Explorer Jacques Cartier, in the 16th century, was the first to describe the acquisition of maple sap. In the early days, most maple sap was made into sugar, which sold for half the cost of imported cane sugar. Maple syrup makes a wonderful contribution to many of our recipes, not just as a topping for pancakes. Once you've tasted the real thing, the fake stuff just doesn't cut it.

½ cup (125 mL) maple syrup

1½ cups (375 mL) brown sugar

3 Tbsp (45 mL) flour

1 cup (250 mL) heavy cream (32%)

1 tsp (5 mL) vanilla

1 Tbsp (15 mL) unsalted butter

pinch of salt

pinch of nutmeg (optional)

½ cup (125 mL) chopped nuts such as pecans or walnuts (optional)

pastry, enough for a single crust (see p. 75 or use purchased)

Preheat oven to 350° F (175° C). In a saucepan over low heat, bring maple syrup, brown sugar, flour and cream to a boil and simmer for about 10 minutes or until thickened. Stir in vanilla, butter and salt. Add nutmeg and nuts, if using. Pour into a prepared pie crust and bake for 30 to 35 minutes.

Let cool to room temperature before serving. Serve with fresh fruit and ice cream.

Birch syrup can be tapped from mature white birch (Betula papyrifera). The flavour is slightly more bitter-sweet and is lighter in colour than maple syrup. Founder of the Alberta Sugarmakers' Association, William Bard hopes to eventually develop birch syrup processing in the province.

At the 2006 Turin Olympics, the Norwegian ski coach Bjornar Hakensmoen gave Alberta skier Sara Renner a ski pole after hers broke, and she and partner Beckie Scott went on to win silver in the team sprint. In gratitude, Canadians sent 7400 cans of maple syrup to Norway, where it is not a common treat. Hakensmoen and Renner led the Calgary Stampede Parade in July 2006.

Ruth's Unbaked Strawberry Cheesecake

Serves 8

The name "strawberry" is derived from the Old English *streawberige*, with *streaw* meaning "straw" and *berige* meaning "berry." In parts of northern Europe, wild berries are still commonly gathered by threading them onto a straw, giving a possible origin for the name. Historically, the strawberries (*Fragaria species*) of Europe were probably not widely eaten—although they were used occasionally for medicine, and the plants did become popular with the French nobility for their flowers. By the 1400s, strawberries were being sold on the streets of London. The importation of a large Chilean species of strawberry to Europe in 1714 was the first step in developing the large strawberries we now know and love. Strawberries, which are ready for harvest by the beginning of July, are a good source of vitamin C. They grow well in our climate and are the first local fruit of the season. Alberta is dotted with U-pick farms that feature strawberries, and they are easy to grow in a container garden on your deck or balcony. This recipe is an unbaked cheesecake, which I find creamier and not as heavy as baked cheesecakes, and it's more suited to the juicy strawberries.

Crust
2 cups (500 mL) graham wafer crumbs

½ cup (125 mL) + 1 Tbsp (15 mL) unsalted butter, melted

zest of 1 lemon, finely chopped

Filling
3 x 250 g packages cream cheese, at room temperature

½ to 1 cup (125 to 250 mL) icing sugar, sifted

fresh lemon juice

⅓ cup (75 mL) whipping cream (32%)

Topping
1 x 8 oz (250 mL) jar of apple jelly

1 lb (500 g) strawberries, whole, washed and stemmed

Preheat oven to 350° F (175° C). Crush graham wafers with a rolling pin or pulse in a food processor to make crumbs. In a mixing bowl, combine the graham wafer crumbs, melted butter and lemon zest. Pat the mixture evenly into a 10-inch (25 cm) pie plate. Bake in the oven 10 minutes. Cool to room temperature. Cover and chill in the refrigerator until ready to fill. Crust can be made a day in advance.

In a food processor, combine cream cheese, icing sugar and a generous squeeze of lemon juice. Mix until smooth and creamy. Transfer into a large mixing bowl.

In a small bowl, beat the whipping cream until light and fluffy, and fold into the cream cheese mixture. Gently fill the chilled graham crust with the creamy filling and chill for at least 3 hours before serving.

To prepare the topping, gently heat the apple jelly until just warm in a small saucepan. In a medium bowl, pour the warm jelly over the strawberries and mix lightly. Arrange the glazed strawberries on top of the cheesecake.

Tip
You can use the bottom of a small glass to help press the graham wafer crumbs evenly on the pie plate.

Rhubarb Pie with a Meringue Crust

Serves 6

For early pioneers, the robust and hardy rhubarb plant supplied essential vitamins and minerals in spring before any berries ripened. Patches of rhubarb can still be found dotting the Alberta landscape where no trace of a farmhouse remains. Indigenous to Asia, rhubarb was first brought to Europe for its medicinal qualities. Marco Polo had a keen interest in rhubarb, and plantings were recorded in Italy as early as 1608. Huge plantations were soon established in Oxfordshire and Bedfordshire, England, where they still grow today. Officially recognized in Europe as a food by the 17th century, rhubarb was known as "pie plant" because it was most often presented as a pie filling and in other desserts. The English brought the first rhubarb to Canada. A member of the buckwheat family, rhubarb is closely related to sorrel. Although rhubarb is technically a vegetable, the stems are used as a fruit in most recipes. Don't eat the leaves— they're poisonous.

1 cup (250 mL) sugar

3 Tbsp (45 mL) flour

1 tsp (5 mL) cinnamon

2 lbs (1 kg) rhubarb, frozen or fresh

1 x 9-inch (23 cm) pie crust, prebaked (or see p. 75 for Great Pie Crust)

Meringue

⅓ cup (60 mL) sugar

1 Tbsp (15 mL) cornstarch

5 egg whites

½ tsp (2 mL) cream of tartar

Mix together sugar, flour and cinnamon in a large bowl. Slice rhubarb into 1-inch (2.5 cm) pieces and add to the flour-sugar mixture and mix until well coated.

In a saucepan over medium heat, cook rhubarb until it is soft and thickened, about 10 minutes. Let cool for at least 30 minutes.

For the meringue, mix sugar and cornstarch in a small bowl. In another bowl, with an electric mixer, beat egg whites until foamy. Add cream of tartar and beat in sugar-cornstarch mixture, one tablespoon at a time, until egg whites are stiff and glossy.

Pour the cooled rhubarb filling into prepared pie crust and spoon meringue gently on top.

Bake the meringue-topped pie at 350° F (175° C) for 10 to 12 minutes, until the meringue is slightly golden.

A friend of mine has a rhubarb plant that is descended from the rhubarb plant her great-grandparents brought over from England in 1907 when they became homesteaders in the Pincher Creek area of Alberta.

Shaved Fennel Salad

Serves 4

Fennel *(Foeniculum vulgare)* is a tender, aromatic perennial herb with a distinct licorice flavour. It is related to dill, and, like its cousin, its seeds, leaves and flowers can all be enjoyed in everything from soups and salads to dessert. It grows well in Alberta, generally peaking in August. Fennel is often mislabeled as anise, a related plant that bears seeds with a sharper licorice flavour, perhaps best known for its starring role in absinthe. A variety of fennel called Florence fennel *(F. vulgare var. azoricum)* grows a swollen stem base that is used as a vegetable, either raw or cooked. Native to southern Europe and parts of Asia, fennel has become naturalized along roadsides in southern Canada. It is best eaten fresh, but the feathery leaves can be frozen for later use in cooked dishes when fennel is out of season.

2 fennel bulbs, shaved paper thin, some fronds reserved for garnish

2 Tbsp (30 mL) extra virgin olive oil

1 Tbsp (15 mL) fresh lemon juice

1 tsp (5 mL) fresh thyme, chopped

¼ cup (60 mL) flat-leafed parsley, chopped

½ cup (125 mL) green olives, sliced

2 oranges, peeled and segmented

1 small red onion, sliced thin

sea salt and freshly ground pepper to taste

In a large bowl, mix all ingredients together and season with salt and pepper. Place on 4 plates, garnish with reserved fronds and serve.

Tip
Use a mandoline or meat slicer to shave the fennel bulbs.

Apple and Quinoa Salad

Serves 6 as a main-course salad

Known as the Mother Grain by the Incas, quinoa is not a grain at all but rather a seed from a plant in the same family as spinach and buckwheat. Native to South America, it is unique in many ways. Each seed is covered with saponin, a bitter natural residue that turns soapy in water and acts as a natural pesticide. Quinoa is higher in protein than any other grain; the United Nations has even classified it as a supercrop because it is such a complete foodstuff. The leaves of the quinoa plant are also edible and are used as a salad green. Quinoa is available in the grain section of large grocery stores and health food stores across Alberta. It is also grown here by Artesian Acres, a farm in Lacombe that specializes in alternative grains such as kamut and spelt.

juice from 1 lemon

⅓ cup (75 mL) apple cider vinegar

½ cup (125 mL) orange juice

⅓ cup (75 mL) canola or sunflower oil

⅓ cup (75 mL) honey

5 cups (1.25 L) cooked quinoa

2 apples, cored and chopped

1 bell pepper, diced small

1 cup (250 mL) fresh corn kernels

½ cup (125 mL) dried cranberries

½ cup (125 mL) currants

1 small red onion, finely chopped

1 cup (250 mL) toasted, chopped pecans

1 cup (250 mL) fresh parsley and mint, chopped

sea salt and freshly ground pepper to taste

Place lemon juice, apple cider vinegar, orange juice, oil and honey in a small bowl and stir to combine. In a large bowl, combine quinoa and all remaining ingredients well, then stir in dressing. Adjust seasonings and refrigerate until ready to serve.

Tip

To cook quinoa, bring 4 cups (1 L) water to a boil in a wide-bottomed pot with a lid. Add a pinch of salt and stir in 2 cups (500 mL) quinoa. Reduce heat to a simmer, cover and cook until all the water is absorbed, about 25 minutes. You can cook any amount of quinoa you like as long as you keep the 2:1 ratio of liquid to grain. It is also worth experimenting with other liquids such as stock or coconut milk.

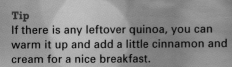

Tip
If there is any leftover quinoa, you can
warm it up and add a little cinnamon and
cream for a nice breakfast.

Highwood Crossing Canola, Tomato and Tempura Bocconcini Salad

Serves 4

In Alberta, canola (*Brassica napus*) is known as liquid gold—and for good reason. It stains summer fields across the province with a blanket of yellow and is Alberta's third most important crop. A distinctly Canadian invention with its home base in Alberta, this member of the cabbage family was developed from rapeseed as a healthier source of vegetable oil in the 1970s. Some 80% of canola grown today has been genetically modified. One source of non-GMO canola is Highwood Crossing, an organic farm in southern Alberta. The farm is the product of the hard work and dedication of the Marshall family, who grow and process everything on their farm to ensure the highest quality. The Marshalls proudly proclaim their cold-pressed organic canola oil to be "Canada's olive oil." It has a fatty acid profile very similar to that of extra-virgin olive oil, with all the healthy omega-3 and omega-6 we need for a good diet.

peanut oil

1 lb (500 g) assorted heirloom tomatoes, sliced into thick rounds

handful fresh basil

17 oz (500 ml) container mini bocconcini, drained and patted very dry

1 recipe of tempura batter (see p. 144)

Highwood Crossing cold-pressed canola oil

juice of 1 lemon

sea salt and freshly ground pepper

Heat peanut oil in pot or deep fryer to 375° F (190° C). Arrange sliced tomato and basil onto individual plates. Dip bocconcini into tempura batter and fry until golden. Serve tempura bocconcini together with tomato slices, drizzle with canola oil and lemon juice. Season with salt and pepper.

Tip
For deep-frying, peanut oil should be 2 to 3 inches (5 to 7.5 cm) deep in pot or use deep fryer according to the manufacturer's directions.

Honey-drizzled Figs with Pecan-crusted Goat Cheese

Serves 6

Be sure to seek out and treat yourself to some of these delicious fruits when they come into season. Fresh figs are available here mostly in fall. Delicate, with a heady sweetness, fresh figs are ripe when they yield to soft pressure, but they have a short shelf life and should be enjoyed within a few days of purchase. If your usual grocer doesn't have them, try Italian or other Mediterranean markets.

1 x 8 oz (250 g) goat cheese log (chèvre)

1 cup (250 mL) toasted, chopped pecans, plus halves for garnish

1 lb (500 g) baby mixed lettuce

⅓ cup (75 mL) extra virgin olive oil

sea salt and freshly ground pepper

12 fresh figs, any variety

½ cup (125 mL) fireweed honey

Roll goat cheese log in nuts, and wrap in cellophane. Refrigerate at least ½ hour and up to 6 hours.

Arrange lettuce onto 6 plates and sprinkle lightly with olive oil. Season with salt and pepper. Cut figs into halves and arrange atop greens.

Slice cheese into 6 equal-sized rounds and place next to figs. Drizzle with honey, season lightly again with salt and pepper and serve.

About 75% of Canada's honey is produced on the Prairies, mostly in Alberta. Fireweed honey, from the provincial flower of the Yukon, is the northernmost honey-nectar flower. It produces a light, mild, floral honey that is highly regarded among honey connoisseurs. Fireweed honey is available from specialty food shops or larger grocery stores. If you can't find it, use any light-coloured, mild honey.

Wild Salmon en Papillote

Serves 4

Although it is not found in Alberta waters, salmon is our most popular seafood choice. We can purchase it from local retailers year-round, but the time to really indulge is during salmon season, which runs from June through September. Wild salmon is always the best choice, even if it costs a bit more, because you get a tastier, leaner and more natural fish. There are five species of wild salmon found in the Pacific: sockeye, pink, chum, chinook, steelhead and coho. Sockeye is the most sought-after salmon variety because of its oil content and rich colour, believed to come from a diet high in shrimp. But many Albertans don't just sit around and wait for this tasty fish to come to the local market—they love to take off to coastal British Columbia for a week's respite, book a salmon fishing charter and stock up on their favourite fish for winter.

4 wild salmon fillets

4 leeks, white parts only, sliced thin and well washed

¼ cup (60 mL) dry white wine

sea salt and freshly ground pepper

1 bunch dill or other fresh herb, chopped

¼ cup (60 mL) unsalted butter, cut into 4 pieces

1 egg white, lightly beaten

1 lemon, sliced

Heat oven to 350° F (175° C). Fold a 24-inch (60 cm) sheet of parchment paper in half, and cut out a heart shape about 4 inches (10 cm) larger than a fish fillet. Place fillet near the fold, and place a handful of leeks next to it, sprinkle with wine, salt, pepper and dill and top with a piece of butter. Brush edges of parchment paper with the egg white, fold paper to enclose fish, and make small overlapping folds to seal the edges, starting at curve of heart. Be sure each fold overlaps the one before it to create an airtight seal. Repeat with rest of fillets. Put packages on a baking sheet, and bake until paper is puffed and brown, about 10 to 15 minutes. Serve salmon in the packets with lemon slices and sautéed vegetables. Be careful of steam when opening the packets.

*Cooking in parchment paper, en papillote in French, is an easy, low-fat way to pre-
pare fish. The word papillote is derived from papillon, meaning butterfly, and hence,
why the parchment pouch is traditionally folded into a heart or butterfly shape.
Try cooking vegetables in parchment as well.*

Blackened Trout with Oven-dried Tomatoes

Serves 2

Even though Alberta is a landlocked province, we love to eat fresh fish here, and trout is definitely at the top of our list. Fresh and frozen trout are available year-round, but prairie folk most frequently indulge in the coral-fleshed fish during the summer. Dozens of trout farms around the province offer U-fish facilities, fish for stocking home ponds and much more. In addition, wild trout are abundant in our province's waterways. These wild fish not only taste great, but are great fun to catch—or catch and release if that is what you prefer. Of the many wild trout found in Alberta's lakes, rivers and steams, the cutthroat and bull are native species. In fact, the bull trout is the provincial fish.

2 lbs (1 kg) Roma tomatoes, halved lengthwise

3 cloves garlic, minced

¼ cup (60 mL) fresh thyme, chopped

sea salt and freshly ground black pepper to taste

½ cup (125 mL) extra virgin olive oil

Spice Mixture

2 tsp (10 mL) paprika

2 tsp (10 mL) chipotle powder or chili powder

2 tsp (10 mL) ground cumin

2 tsp (10 mL) dried thyme

1 tsp (5 mL) freshly ground black pepper

1 tsp (5 mL) sea salt

2 fresh trout, gutted but whole

2 Tbsp (30 mL) canola oil

Preheat the oven to 250° F (120° C).

Scoop out seeds from the tomatoes. Mix the garlic with the thyme, salt and pepper and olive oil. Place the tomatoes cut side up in a roasting pan and drizzle with the garlic mixture. Bake for at least 3 hours or until the tomatoes are dehydrated but still chewy.

Mix all the spices together in a bowl.

Rinse trout with water and pat dry with paper towels. Brush oil on the trout and rub the spice mixture all over.

Heat a heavy-bottomed skillet until it is smoking hot. Place the prepared trout in the skillet and cook for 2 to 4 minutes and turn over. Cook until the trout is firm and cooked through, 3 to 4 minutes. To test doneness, the fish should flake easily with a fork but should not be dry. Serve with oven-dried tomatoes on the side.

Tip
Oven-drying tomatoes is a great way to preserve these tasty bits of summer sunshine. Grow tomatoes in your garden or in containers, or pick them up at farmers' markets.

Tip
Any leftover tomatoes can be covered in olive oil and stored in a jar. They will keep for up to 3 weeks refrigerated.

Grilled Beef Tenderloin with Sautéed Chanterelles

Serves 4

The Canadian cattle industry began in the 1850s in what is now British Columbia and made its way into the southeastern foothills of Alberta in the 1870s, when the North-West Mounted Police arrived to sweep the American whiskey traders out of the West. Southern Alberta is a naturally suitable climate for ranching, with its many streams, sheltered valleys and Chinook winds. Today, the cattle industry is huge—it contributes over 15 billion dollars annually to Canada's economy. What could be better than Alberta beef cooked on a barbecue on a hot summer day!

4 beef tenderloin medallions, about 6 to 8 oz (170 to 250 g) each

olive oil, for brushing

2 tsp (10 mL) kosher salt

freshly ground black pepper

Mushrooms

1 to 2 Tbsp (15 to 30 mL) olive oil

3 shallots, sliced

1 lb (500 g) fresh chanterelles

1 clove garlic, minced

½ cup (125 mL) white wine

1 cup (250 mL) parsley, chopped

¼ cup (60 mL) chives, chopped

sea salt and freshly ground black pepper

Remove beef medallions from refrigerator 15 minutes before cooking.

To prepare the mushrooms, heat olive oil in a skillet over medium-high heat and sauté the shallots until soft. Add chanterelles, garlic and continue to sauté for 5 to 7 minutes, then add white wine and cook until the liquid evaporates. Remove from heat and stir in parsley and chives. Season with salt and pepper.

Prepare a grill or a stove-top grill pan with a medium-high heat fire. Brush beef lightly with olive oil and season with salt and pepper and place on the grill and cook, without moving it, until nice grill marks appear, about 4 minutes. Turn the medallions and continue to grill until an instant-read thermometer inserted into the medallions sideways registers about 120° F (50° C), about 3 to 4 minutes more. Set aside on a cutting board to rest for 5 minutes before serving.

Divide medallions among plates and spoon on the mushrooms.

Mo-Na Food Enterprises of Edmonton, which bills itself as "The First Canadian Wild Mushroom Company," offers a variety of mushroom products, including chanterelles and morels.

Mu Shu Duck with Peaches and Daikon

Serves 4

Game birds such as geese, wild turkey, prairie chicken, partridge and grouse were an important food source for Canada's indigenous peoples, and early Alberta settlers soon learned to hunt them as well. Game birds have always been abundant here, at least seasonally; probably the best-known duck, the mallard (*Anas platyrhynchos*), is also Alberta's most common duck. Green Eggs and Ham, a family-run mixed farm located between Leduc and Wetaskiwin, offers, among other specialties, free-range duck and eggs. Their duck is available at the farm gate, farmers' markets and many retail outlets, as well as on the menus of Alberta's finer restaurants.

Duck

8 oz (250 g) duck breast, about 2 breasts, cut into strips

3 Tbsp (45 mL) rice vinegar

2 Tbsp (30 mL) soy sauce

1 tsp (5 mL) sesame oil

1 Tbsp (15 mL) garlic, minced

1 Tbsp (15 mL) fresh ginger, finely chopped

grape seed or canola oil for stir frying

½ cup (125 mL) green onions, finely sliced

Daikon

1 daikon radish, 4-inch piece, grated

1 Tbsp (15 mL) rice vinegar

½ tsp (2 mL) sugar

1 Tbsp (15 mL) green onion, finely sliced

In a bowl, toss the duck with the rice vinegar, soy sauce, sesame oil, garlic and ginger. Cover and marinate, refrigerated, for 2 hours. In another bowl, toss the daikon with rice vinegar, sugar and green onion. Set aside.

Heat a splash of grape seed oil in a wok (or heavy-bottomed pan) and add the marinated duck strips. Stir fry over high heat until

browned and cooked through, about 3 minutes. Remove from the pan, toss with green onions and set aside. Reduce the heat to medium and cook peaches in the wok for 5 minutes, set aside. Add a splash of oil to the wok and cook eggs, sunny side up.

Serve duck, daikon, peaches, eggs, enoki mushrooms on a platter along with side serving plates. Spread a spoonful of hoisin sauce on a flatbread and place some meat, peaches and vegetables on top, roll up and enjoy.

2 fresh peaches, cut into eighths

4 large eggs

4 oz (125 g) fresh enoki mushrooms

hoisin sauce

1 package store-bought flatbread, such as chapati

Barley and Lentil Burgers

Serves 4

It is believed that barley was first cultivated in the Middle East 9000 years ago. Explorer Christopher Columbus brought it to North America from Europe, and today it is the third largest crop in Alberta after wheat and canola. Canada is the second largest barley producer in the world, with about 12 million tons (11 million tonnes) produced annually. Barley is an invaluable crop in Alberta: about half of all the barley grown in Canada comes from Alberta. Most of Alberta's barley is used to feed cattle, and the rest is used for malting and human consumption. Barley is a very healthy grain. It has low gluten, is high in B vitamins and is an excellent source of dietary fibre. Barley is also blessed with a low glycemic index, which is important to a diabetic diet. Hamilton's Barley Flour in Olds is a family farm dedicated to providing Albertans with excellent whole grain barley flour.

1 x 19 oz (540 ml) can lentils

½ cup (125 mL) cooked barley

1 small carrot, grated

1 egg

1 Tbsp (15 mL) ketchup

⅓ cup (75 mL) dry bread crumbs

1 small onion, finely chopped

1 clove garlic, minced

1 Tbsp (15 mL) thyme, chopped

salt and freshly ground pepper to taste

dash hot pepper sauce (optional)

1 to 2 Tbsp (15 to 30 mL) canola or sunflower oil

Place lentils, barley and carrot in a medium bowl and mix well (your hands work best for this). Stir in egg, ketchup, bread crumbs, onion, garlic and thyme, salt and pepper and if using, hot pepper sauce. Cover and refrigerate for 1 hour.

Shape lentil mixture into four ½-inch-thick (1 cm) patties. Heat oil in a skillet over medium heat and cook patties until browned on each side. Alternatively, brush patties with oil and grill until browned, about 5 minutes for each side. Serve on buns with your favourite condiments.

Tip
To cook barley, use 3:1 ratio of water to barley. A ¼ cup (60 mL) of pearl barley makes about 1 cup (250 mL) of cooked barley. Bring water and barley to a boil and reduce to a simmer for 30 to 45 minutes, until barley is soft.

Canada Malting in southeast Calgary is the world's largest producer of malt. Every year, it uses about 385,000 tons (350,000 tonnes) of barley from Alberta growers to produce fine malt for local and export markets. The malt is important not only to the local economy, but also to the cattle industry and the many local microbreweries.

Eggplant Lasagna

Serves 6 to 8

Eggplant (*Solanum melongena*), like its cousin the tomato, was long believed to be poisonous (well, more accurately, thought to drive people mad) and got off to a slow start in gardens outside of the Mediterranean, except as an ornamental plant. Eggplant is unique in the nightshade family as the only member to have originated in the Eastern Hemisphere—in India and China specifically. Like tomatoes, peppers and potatoes, eggplants come in a wide variety of shapes and colours, although globe-shaped varieties such as "Black Beauty" are most common in grocery stores here. Eggplants need a lot of sun and heat to grow, so most Alberta farms grow their eggplants in hothouses to secure a reliable supply. By the way, eggplant got its name because early varieties introduced to Europe were white and looked like eggs!

1 large eggplant, sliced ½ inch (1 cm) thick, crosswise

1 medium zucchini, sliced ½ inch (1 cm) thick

2 to 3 Tbsp (30 to 45 mL) olive oil

2 Tbsp (30 mL) butter

Tomato Sauce

1 Tbsp (15 mL) olive oil

2 large onions, finely chopped

3 or 4 cloves garlic, minced

2 bay leaves

splash of red wine

2 cups (500 mL) canned plum tomatoes, roughly chopped

12 sheets oven-ready lasagna noodles

2 cups freshly grated Asiago cheese

sea salt and freshly ground pepper to taste

Toss eggplant and zucchini slices with olive oil and season with salt and pepper. Grill on a stovetop grill or barbecue for 5 minutes on each side. Set aside.

Preheat oven to 375° F (190° C). Warm oil and butter in a heavy-based casserole over medium heat. Add onion and sauté for about 5 minutes until softened and translucent. Add garlic and cook for another couple of minutes, stirring to coat well. Cook gently for about 5 minutes. Add bay leaves, salt and pepper. Pour in wine and simmer until it has evaporated, then add tomatoes with their juice and stir thoroughly. Cook, uncovered, for 30 minutes. Taste and correct seasoning.

For ricotta mixture, combine ingredients in medium bowl. Season to taste and set aside.

For béchamel, pour milk into a saucepan with bay leaves, onion and a generous pinch of nutmeg. Bring to just below the boiling point, then remove from heat and leave to infuse for 10 minutes. Strain the milk to remove the bay leaves and onion.

Melt butter in a saucepan and stir in the flour. Cook, stirring, for 5 minutes. Pour the hot milk into the flour mixture. Cook on low heat, stirring frequently, for 10 minutes until thickened. Season the sauce with salt and pepper and set aside.

To assemble, start by buttering a 13 x 9 x 3-inch (33 x 23 x 5 cm) baking pan. Pour some béchamel into the baking pan—enough to just cover the bottom. Top with a layer of lasagna, add béchamel, a layer of grilled vegetables, tomato sauce, then more béchamel and a good handful of Asiago cheese. Cover with lasagna, then the ricotta mixture. Top with lasagna, then béchamel, vegetables, tomato sauce. Add another layer of lasagna and top with béchamel. Add a final sprinkling of Asiago cheese. Bake for 30 to 40 minutes, until browned and bubbling all over.

Tip

Older eggplants will have an acrid flavour, so choose freshly picked, if possible. Alternatively, you can remove most of the bitter flavour by salting the sliced eggplant and letting it sit for 10 to 15 minutes. Gently squeeze out the bitter liquid, rinse lightly in cold water and pat dry on paper towel.

Tip

You can add as many layers as you wish, depending on the size of your pan.

Ricotta Mixture

2 cups (500 g) ricotta cheese

½ cup (125 mL) freshly grated Parmesan cheese

½ cup (125 mL) freshly grated Mozzarella cheese

sea salt and freshly ground pepper

Béchamel

3 cups (750 mL) milk

2 bay leaves

1 onion, halved

pinch of freshly grated nutmeg

¼ cup (60 mL) butter

¼ cup (60 mL) flour

sea salt and freshly ground pepper

Summer Squash Ratatouille

Serves 4 as a main course, 6 as a side dish

The difference between summer squash and winter squash is in their shelf life. Winter squash, such as pumpkins, develop hard rinds and can be stored for months, whereas summer squash, such as zucchini, are best eaten before they mature and develop a bitter flavour. You can grow both types in your garden, and squash grows well in Alberta, so you will need many delicious recipes to use them all up. Most squash are ready in about 50 days from sowing to harvest. Early Native peoples in North and South America discovered that members of the squash family *(Cucurbitaceae)* love to cross-pollinate, giving them abundant and interesting varieties to choose from. Grown as part of their "Three Sisters" diet, along with corn and beans, squash was crossbred in hopes of producing larger seeds and flesh that was less bitter.

1 medium eggplant, 2½ lbs (1.2 kg), cut into ½ in (1 cm) cubes

olive oil for cooking

1 lb (500 g) assorted summer squash, as much variety as possible, cut into ½ in (1 cm) slices

2 medium onions, sliced

2 red bell peppers, seeded and cut into ½ in (1 cm) strips

3 ripe but firm tomatoes about 1 lb (500 g), seeded and quartered

2 cloves garlic, minced

⅓ cup (75 mL) of a mixture of chopped fresh rosemary, thyme, basil, fennel and marjoram

pinch of dried lavender

sea salt and freshly ground black pepper to taste

French bread

Lay the eggplant cubes on paper towels and sprinkle with salt. Let them sit for 15 minutes, then rinse and pat dry.

Have a large bowl ready. Heat a splash of olive oil in a large skillet or casserole over medium heat. Add the eggplant chunks and cook until they start to soften, remove from pan and set aside in the bowl to make room for the next vegetable. Add more olive oil, as needed, and continue with the squash, onions and peppers separately.

Return all vegetables to pan; add tomatoes, garlic and herbs. Season with salt and pepper and stir to mix. Simmer over medium heat until much of the liquid is evaporated, about 10 minutes, then cover, turn heat to medium low and cook until the vegetables are tender, about 45 minutes to 1 hour, stirring occasionally to prevent sticking. Serve at room temperature with crusty French bread.

Tip
Squash blossoms are also edible and make a great vessel for stuffing and deep frying. Make sure you choose the male stems (but leave a few for pollination) and leave the fruit-bearing females for an abundant summer supply.

Char-grilled Taber Corn with Jalapeño Lime Butter

Taber is the "Corn Capital of Canada" and proud home to the annual "Cornfest" in August. Taber receives more sunlight during the year than any other region in Canada, and its hot summer days and cooler nights provide optimal conditions for bringing up the sugar content in corn. As a result of its climate, soil type and use of irrigation, the Taber area is renown for growing the sweetest corn. Corn *(Zea mays)* is native to the Americas, and its history dates back thousands of years. The first corn was probably a popcorn variety, and it wasn't until its introduction to the European settlers that sweet corn strains started to emerge. Sadly, in the quest for sweet corn, we have lost many of the hundreds of varieties that were once common. Corn is really a grain, though we generally eat it fresh, as a vegetable. One of the most sought-after varieties of sweet corn is "Simonet," a variety developed by Robert Simonet of Edmonton.

ears of Taber corn

jalapeño lime butter (see below)

lime wedges

sea salt to taste

Preheat the barbecue to medium-high heat. Peel back the husks, leaving them attached, and remove the silk from the corn. Rewrap, tying with butcher twine or kitchen string if necessary. Barbecue for about 10 minutes, turning to cook all sides. If husks start to burn, spritz with water.

Serve hot corn with rounds of the jalapeño lime butter, lime wedges and sea salt.

Jalapeño Lime Butter

1 cup (250 mL) unsalted butter, softened

1 jalapeño pepper, seeded and finely chopped

zest from 1 lime

1 clove garlic, minced

1 tsp (5 mL) sea salt

Jalapeño Lime Butter

Mix the ingredients together in a bowl or in a food processor. Wrap in plastic and shape into a cylinder about an inch (2.5 cm) in diameter, and refrigerate.

Tip
To keep the sugars from turning to starch, keep freshly picked corn as cool as possible and enjoy it soon after harvesting. Fresh corn can be steamed, boiled or grilled, and older corn can be cut from the cob and added to soups and stews.

Oven-roasted Quince

Serves 4

It is unfortunate for us that our summers are not hot enough for the beautifully perfumed quince *(Cydonia oblonga)* to fully ripen here. In fact, most quince found in Alberta groceries comes from Argentina. Look for this treat in late summer. Quince is a relative of the apple and is native to Persia and Greece, although it was the Greeks who first cultivated this fruit as we know it today. It is believed that many historical accounts of the apple, such as in the Garden of Eden, actually refer to the quince. Quince is most often eaten cooked because otherwise it is too sour and hard. It can only be consumed raw if it has been softened by frost.

2 large quince, peeled and halved

2 cups (500 mL) honey

2 cups (500 mL) water

½ cup (125 mL) orange juice

1 vanilla bean, halved and split

Cinnamon Ice Cream

2 cups (500 mL) best quality vanilla ice cream

2 Tbsp (30 mL) ground cinnamon

Preheat oven to 275° F (135° C). Combine ingredients in an ovenproof dish and bring to a boil on the stovetop. Cover with a piece of parchment paper and weigh down with a small plate. Bake in oven for 3 hours, turning once during cooking.

Remove from oven and let cool. Store quince refrigerated in the syrup for up to 6 months.

To serve, pour syrup into a small pot and reduce it until it becomes a deep red, then toss the quince in the syrup to coat. Serve with Cinnamon Ice Cream.

Cinnamon Ice Cream
In an electric mixer or food processor, combine ice cream with cinnamon.

Mix to combine, then freeze until set.

Vanilla beans can used to infuse sugar with its wonderful aroma and flavour. Cut a vanilla bean in half lengthwise (or dry and reuse the pods from the recipe) and cover with 1 to 2 cups of white sugar for 3 to 4 weeks or more, stirring once a week. You can use vanilla sugar in your coffee or tea, or add it to whipped cream.

Onion Jam

Onions are extremely versatile to have on hand. You can use them raw, sautéed, caramelized and deep-fried, and there are many types of onions available in Alberta. Red onions are usually used in Greek salads, and white and yellow onions are ubiquitous. This is a recipe for savoury jam, suitable for serving with meats such as roast beef. I paired it here with a cheese and crackers tray as part of an after-dinner treat, but it works equally well as an appetizer.

4 Tbsp olive oil

6 medium sweet onions, sliced thinly

pinch sea salt

1 Tbsp balsamic vinegar

¼ cup port

sprig of fresh thyme

½ cup muscovado sugar

1 tsp mustard seeds

½ tsp red pepper flakes

¼ cup tomato, finely chopped

Melt the oil in heavy frying pan. Add the onions and sauté until slightly brown. Season with salt. Reduce the heat, then continue to cook, stirring constantly, until caramelized and tender. Add the remaining ingredients, except the tomato, and cook on low heat for 30 minutes stirring occasionally. Add the tomato and cook for 15 more minutes. Let cool and store in a jar in the refrigerator. Keeps for 2 weeks refrigerated.

Try onion jam on pizzas and sandwiches.

Iced Tea with Fresh Mint

Serves 4

Across Alberta, there are at least 50 tearooms that serve a variety of teas, both iced and hot. Although Albertans love their coffee, tea is gaining popularity as we strive for a healthier lifestyle, and sipping afternoon tea at the local teahouse is becoming a favourite pastime. Traditionally, iced tea was served as a refreshing punch spiked with alcohol. The version we think of most often today, a freshly brewed tea sweetened and flavoured with lemon, first became popular after being served at the 1904 St. Louis World's Fair. Iced tea can be made with any tea you like, from the standard black tea to green tea and even caffeine-free herbal tea and rooibos.

6 cups (1.5 L) cold water

5 level tsp (25 mL) good quality, loose tea

⅔ cup (150 mL) white sugar, or to taste

1 handful of fresh mint, rinsed and patted dry

1 lime or lemon

Bring 4 cups (1 L) of water to a boil. Place the tea in a pitcher and pour the boiling water over the tea. Let infuse for 30 minutes.

Stir in sugar to dissolve and strain tea into a clean pitcher. Add the remaining water.

Bruise the mint by crushing it lightly with a rolling pin or the bottom of a glass and place in the pitcher.

Chill tea for at least 1 hour. Remove mint before serving, and serve with a wedge of lime or lemon and a sprig of mint, if desired.

Some people call the alcohol-spiked version of iced tea "iced tea on a stick." Iced coffee is also a popular summer drink available homemade or purchased from fine coffee shops throughout the province.

Bles-Wold Yogurt and Honey Semifreddo

Serves 4 to 6

Tinie Eilers and Hennie Bos had over 20 years of dairy experience in the Netherlands. In 1994 they decided to move to central Alberta and start a dairy farm, and are we ever lucky they did! Tinie started to make a luscious and naturally low-fat yogurt as a hobby, and Bles-Wold yogurt has become both a staple in many Alberta households and an icon in the dairy community. With a focus on all-natural products and sustainable farming practices, Bles-Wold now has a herd of 200 purebred and free-range Holstein cows. They offer Albertans a truly fresh product—three or four days from cow to table. Bles-Wold yogurt and sour cream is available at markets throughout the province and at their farm in Lacombe.

2¼ cups heavy cream (32%)

5 egg yolks

½ cup honey

½ cup unflavoured yogurt

In a mixer, whisk cream to stiff peaks. Transfer the whipped cream into another bowl and set aside. Clean and dry the mixing bowl and whisk yolks with honey until pale yellow and thickened. Fold in yogurt. Then fold in whipped cream.

Line a mold with plastic wrap. Add the filling into the mold. Cover and freeze for 24 hours. Remove semifreddo from the freezer just before serving. Top with your favourite berries.

Semifreddo is Italian for "half-cold" and describes the half-frozen or chilled nature of this delicious confection.

Saskatoon Pie

Serves 6

People who grew up in Alberta have fond memories of secret saskatoon patches and the bountiful harvests that lasted all winter long. The saskatoon (*Amelanchier alnifolia,* also called serviceberry and juneberry), which is related to cherries and apples, is also an essential winter food for wildlife. Although most prolific on the Prairies, the saskatoon grows from coast to coast and is a truly Canadian berry, but to many Eastern Canadians, it remains a mystery. Interior B.C. and Plains First Nations peoples, however, have been enjoying them for centuries in everything from pemmican to porridge and, of course, freshly picked. The name "saskatoon" is believed to be a shortened form of the Cree or Blackfoot name for this berry. In Britain, saskatoons were pulled off the shelves in June 2004, after their safety was questioned because there was no history of people eating the berries in Europe!

pastry, enough for a double crust (see opposite, or use purchased)

1 egg white, beaten, for brushing pastry

6 cups (1.5 L) fresh saskatoons

¼ cup (60 mL) cornstarch

1 cup (250 mL) unbleached sugar

juice of ⅓ lemon

pinch of sea salt

1 Tbsp (15 mL) unsalted butter

2 Tbsp (30 mL) heavy cream (32%), for top of crust

¼ cup (60 mL) unbleached sugar, for top of crust

Preheat oven to 400° F (200° C). Roll pastry out and use 1 to line a pie plate. Brush inside of bottom crust with egg white to prevent juices from soaking in and making it soggy. Pick over saskatoons and toss together in a large bowl with cornstarch, sugar, lemon juice and salt. Pour into crust and dot with butter. Secure top crust, and be sure to cut air vents. Brush with cream and sprinkle with unbleached sugar. Bake for 12 minutes. Turn heat down to 365° F (185° C) and bake 20 to 30 minutes until crust is golden brown and filling is bubbly. Place on a wire rack to cool for at least 1 hour.

Great Pie Crust

Mix flour, salt and sugar in a bowl. Using your cheese grater, grate frozen butter into flour mixture. Toss lightly to distribute butter and add lemon juice and enough water for dough just to come together. Divide in half, wrap each piece in plastic wrap and flatten into a disc. Chill for at least 30 minutes before using. Makes enough for a double-crusted pie.

2½ cups (625 mL) flour

1 tsp (5 mL) sea salt

1 Tbsp (15 mL) sugar

1 cup (250 mL) unsalted butter, frozen

1 Tbsp (15 mL) lemon juice

about ⅓ cup (75 mL) ice water

Tip

For individual free-form pies, as shown below, simply divide pastry into 6 equal portions, roll out to ⅛ inch (0.25 cm) and lay out on a baking sheet lined with parchment paper. Brush with egg white and divide filling evenly onto rounds, leaving a 1-inch (2.5 cm) border. Fold border up over filling, leaving centre open. Dot fruit with butter, brush pastry with cream and sprinkle with unbleached sugar. Follow baking instructions as opposite, reducing baking time to about 15 minutes.

Currant Cooler

Serves 2

Currants are members of the genus *Ribes,* which includes the edible currants (black currant, red currant and white currant) along with gooseberries and many ornamental plants. They are native to the temperate regions of the Northern Hemisphere and grow well in Alberta. Black currants are the most popular variety grown here, with several hundred hectares dedicated to this berry. Black currants produce more juice per hectare than oranges and are also higher in vitamin C. Currants are at their peak in August and are available at many U-pick farms around the province. They also make a beautiful fruit-bearing shrub for any yard.

6 oz (180 mL) currant juice

4 oz (120 mL) frozen vodka

3 drops dry vermouth

frozen currants for garnish

2 martini glasses

ice

Fill shaker ½ full of ice. Pour in vodka, dry vermouth and currant juice. Shake and strain. Pour into martini glasses and garnish with frozen currants.

Vodka is best kept in the freezer, so it's ready for use in your favourite cocktails.

Raspberry Tart

Serves 6 to 8

Fragrantly sweet and subtly tart, raspberries (*Rubus* spp.) are a favourite Alberta fruit. A member of the rose family, raspberries can be grown anywhere in the province, although it is slightly more difficult to grow them in the Chinook belt of southern Alberta. The wild raspberry (*R. idaeus*) occurs naturally in parts of the province and produces a smaller but equally delicious berry. Raspberries are healthy, antioxidant-rich berries, high in ellagic acid—the same family of tannins that make wine, green tea and fruit, such as pomegranates, an important part of a healthy lifestyle. Raspberries are also an excellent source of manganese, vitamin C and dietary fibre, and the leaves make a soothing herbal tea.

Crust

1¼ cups (310 mL) all-purpose flour

¼ cup (60 mL) sugar

½ cup (125 mL) or 1 stick unsalted butter, cold and cut into pieces

2 to 3 Tbsp (30 to 45 mL) cold water

Filling

2 x 8 oz containers (275 g) mascarpone, room temperature

½ cup (125 mL) sugar

1 tsp (5 mL) vanilla

3 cups (750 mL) raspberries, picked over

Glaze

1 x 8 oz (250 mL) jar of apple jelly

For the crust, place flour, sugar and butter in a food processor and blend until mixture resembles coarse meal. Add 2 Tbsp (30 mL) of the water until incorporated. Add enough remaining water, if necessary, until mixture comes together but is still crumbly. Wrap dough in plastic and refrigerate for 1 hour.

Preheat oven to 350° F (175° C). Press crust mixture evenly onto bottom and sides of an 11-inch (28 cm) tart pan with removable fluted rim or 6 to 8 individual tart tins. Prick crust with a fork, line it with parchment and weigh it down with pie weights or dried beans. Bake in middle of oven until golden, about 15 minutes. Let cool to room temperature and chill for 1 hour in refrigerator.

Make the filling while the crust chills. In a bowl, using an electric mixer, beat mascarpone, sugar and vanilla together until smooth. Pour filling into chilled crust, spreading evenly, and arrange raspberries on top.

If keeping the tart longer than one day, brush raspberries lightly with a glaze of warmed apple jelly.

Tip
When out picking raspberries in your yard or favourite U-pick farm, be sure to keep them as cool as possible, and store them unwashed. Ideally, pick them during cooler times of the day or on a cloudy day.

Mascarpone is a rich cream cheese that has the consistency of a stiff whipped cream. Originally produced in the Lombardy region of Italy, it is now available in grocery stores and Italian markets.

Blueberry Ice Cream

Makes 4 cups (1 L)

Blueberries, which grow across much of the country, were a significant food source for Canada's Native peoples, and parts of the plant were also important in medical uses. About half of Canada's commercial blueberry harvest comes from cultivated highbush varieties (*Vaccinium corymbosum*), and the rest is supplied by managed stands of wild lowbush berries (*V. angustifolium* and *V. myrtilloides*). In Alberta, wild blueberries grow in the northern part of the province on the Taiga Plains, an area well suited to shrubs such as the blueberry and cranberry. "Wild blues" are smaller, with a deeper blue colour and more intense blueberry flavour than the cultivated berries. Canada is the world's largest supplier of lowbush blueberries. Bursting with flavour, full of antioxidants and containing very few calories, blueberries are said to be among the healthiest of foods.

1 cup (250 mL) whole milk (3%)

3 cups (750 mL) heavy cream (32%)

1 vanilla bean, split lengthwise

5 egg yolks

¾ cup (175 mL) sugar

2½ cups (625 mL) washed blueberries

In a heavy-bottomed saucepan, heat milk, cream and vanilla bean until just before boiling, stirring occasionally. Remove from heat, and take out vanilla bean and scrape out the seeds adding them to the milk. Set aside.

In a mixing bowl, whisk the egg yolks and sugar until pale yellow and thickened. Slowly pour about one cup of the hot mixture into the egg yolks, whisking constantly. Add the yolk mixture back into the rest of the cream and cook over medium heat, stirring constantly, until the mixture thickens and coats the back of a spoon. Be sure not to let the mixture boil at any time or it will curdle. Pour through a fine strainer into a bowl, add blueberries and freeze in an ice cream maker according to the manufacturer's instructions.

Many adults fondly remember the ice cream sold by vendors travelling the streets of their neighbourhoods during long, hot summer days of their childhood. Even today when the familiar music is heard wafting through open windows, it makes us all want to "scream for ice cream."

Yogurt with Flaxseed and Maple Syrup

Serves 1

Alberta is the third largest flax producer in Canada, and the country is a world leader in flax exports. This plant, which is one of only a few plants that sport truly blue flowers, has been grown since ancient times for both its nutritious seeds and its fibre, from which fine linen is made. Louis Hébert, the first farmer in what is now Canada, brought flax *(Linum usitatissimum)* to New France in 1617. Flaxseeds are the most concentrated vegetable source of omega-3 fatty acid and are among the very best sources of both soluble and insoluble dietary fibre. Flaxseeds are used in many products; they may be whole, ground or pressed into oil. They are used in baking and pet food; they are even a popular addition to the diet of laying hens producing omega-3-enriched "designer eggs."

This really isn't a recipe, but rather a list of ingredients that are tasty together as well as being healthy for you. Flaxseeds have a lovely nutty flavour, in addition to thickening the yogurt. I use 2 Tbsp (30 mL) of flaxseed, but you can add any amount you like.

1 cup (250 mL) plain yogurt
ground golden flaxseed
pure maple syrup to taste
fresh fruit of your choice

Mix yogurt, flaxseed and maple syrup together and garnish with fruit.

Here's something I'll bet you didn't know: 1 Tbsp (15 mL) of ground flaxseeds and ¼ cup (60 ml) of water = 1 egg. Well, it replaces an egg in most baking, such as cakes and cookies, but the substitution doesn't work for foods such as meringues or omelettes.

Fruit Smoothie

Serves 1

Berries were an important part of the Plains natives' lives long before the first Europeans came to Alberta. Berries were eaten fresh, dried or preserved in oil. They were used for dyes, medicine and even jewellery. Learning to use indigenous foods such as berries often sustained early settlers during their first months in Canada. Today, Alberta has some 300 fruit and berry growers and over 1000 hectares (over 2500 acres) of land devoted to the industry. The most common types of native Alberta berries are saskatoons, raspberries, strawberries, chokecherries and cranberries. New species, such as the honeyberry *(Lonicera kamchatika;* edible honeysuckle) from Siberia, are being introduced regularly, and new winter-hardy varieties of fruits such as cherries are being successfully grown on farms such as Orchard Palace near Brosseau, Alberta.

1 banana, peeled and frozen

¾ cup (175 mL) fresh or frozen berries

¼ cup (60 mL) coconut milk

1 cup (250 mL) vanilla soy milk

1 Tbsp (15 mL) almond butter

¼ cup (60 mL) crushed ice

Purée all ingredients in a blender until smooth.

Tip
Coconut milk from a can will keep in the fridge for 4–5 days.

Dr. Ieuan Evans is an Albertan known for his work on breeding and evaluating fruit tree varieties for the Prairies. The Evans Cherry, which has sold some 3 million trees, is named for him.

Spiced Parsnip and Cauliflower Soup

Serves 4 to 6

With its elegant ivory colour and sweet, complex flavour, the parsnip *(Pastinaca sativa)* is the queen of root vegetables. It can be used in everything from soups to main courses, and when combined with some melted butter and brown sugar or honey for a side dish, it tastes just like candy. A favourite throughout Europe, the parsnip has been cultivated there since medieval times. Although it came to North America in the 17th century, the parsnip has never gained great popularity here in Alberta. This situation is unfortunate, given that this root crop is especially well suited to a short growing season in a cool climate such as Alberta's. The parsnip is best eaten late in autumn, once it has benefited from exposure to frost. Unlike its cousin the carrot, the parsnip has no vitamin A, but it has more vitamin C.

2 to 3 Tbsp (15 to 30 mL) olive oil

1 Tbsp (15 mL) yellow mustard seeds

2 onions, finely chopped

2 garlic cloves, minced

1 tsp (5 mL) fresh ginger, finely chopped

1 Tbsp (15 mL) turmeric

1 tsp (5 mL) cardamom

1 tsp (5 mL) cumin

1 lb (500 g) cauliflower, trimmed and cut into florets

1 lb (500 g) parsnips, peeled and cut into chunks roughly the same size as the cauliflower

2 cups (500 mL) vegetable or chicken stock or water

1²/₃ cups (400 mL) coconut milk

sea salt and freshly ground pepper to taste

1 Tbsp (15 mL) fresh cilantro finely chopped

Heat the oil in a large saucepan over medium-high heat. When the oil is hot, add the mustard seeds and cook until they begin to pop. Add onion, garlic and ginger, and cook for a couple of minutes until the onion is soft and translucent. Add turmeric, cardamom and cumin. Add cauliflower and parsnip and cook the mixture while stirring for a couple of minutes. Add the stock or water to the pan and bring it slowly to a boil. Skim off any scum that comes to the top and reduce the soup to a simmer. Leave it to cook gently for 30 minutes, stirring it regularly.

The soup is ready when the cauliflower is cooked and tender. Stir in the coconut milk. Purée the soup until smooth and return it to a clean saucepan. Season the soup with salt and pepper, garnish with cilantro and serve.

Tip
Parsnips are best stored in a very cold location or in the refrigerator.

For a different snack, try making parsnip chips! Peel 3 or 4 parsnips lengthwise with a sharp vegetable peeler into long paper thin strips, until you've reached the central core. Heat oil in a medium-sized saucepan to 350° F (175° C) and drop parsnip strips in small batches and fry for 1 minute until crisp and golden. Drain on paper towels, season with sea salt and serve.

Curried Pumpkin Soup

Serves 4 to 6

If Taber is the "Corn Capital of Canada," then Smoky Lake is the heart of all things pumpkin (Cucurbita pepo). The "Great White North Pumpkin Fair and Weigh-Off" is held annually on the first Saturday of October. In 2006 the winning pumpkin weighed 1029 pounds (about 468 kilograms) and was grown by Don Crews in Lloydminster—and it took 11 men to move. The competition featured 89 entries, with 17,400 pounds (7900 kilograms) of pumpkin. The town even features a 12,000-pound (5443-kilogram) concrete pumpkin. Pumpkins and other squashes are New World plants that humans have cultivated as food crops for at least 7000 years. The flesh was consumed raw or roasted, the flowers and seeds were sometimes eaten and the skins could be cut into strips, dried and made into mats. Pumpkin is a nutritious winter vegetable high in vitamin C. For people who support and buy locally produced food, look out for great pumpkins in farmers' markets in fall.

splash of olive oil

2 medium yellow onions, finely chopped

2 cloves garlic, finely chopped

1 tsp (5 mL) mustard seed

1 piece of fresh ginger, 1-inch (2.5 cm) wide, peeled and finely chopped

vegetable or chicken stock or water, enough to cover vegetables

1 tsp (5 mL) turmeric

3 lbs (1.5 kg) sugar pumpkin, peeled, seeded and cut into bite-sized chunks

1 small handful cilantro leaves, finely chopped

1⅔ cups (400 mL) coconut milk

sea salt and freshly ground pepper to taste

Heat the oil in a medium pot over medium-high heat. When the oil is hot, add the onion, garlic, mustard seeds and ginger and cook for a couple of minutes until the onion is soft and translucent. Add pumpkin chunks to the pot and cook for a couple of minutes while stirring. Add stock or water and turmeric and bring slowly to a boil. Skim off any scum that comes to the top and reduce the soup to a simmer. Cook gently for at least 20 minutes, stirring occasionally.

When the pumpkin is tender, remove from heat and purée one-third of the soup with the coconut milk in a blender or food processor. Return to the pot. Bring back to a simmer and season with salt and pepper. Serve hot, garnished with the cilantro sprinkled on top.

Pumpkins aren't the only vegetables that have been carved at Halloween. Beets and turnips have also been at the sharp end of a carver's knife, although these days it's hard to imagine a Halloween beet touching our hearts the same way a carved pumpkin does.

Chicken and Mushroom Pot Pie

Serves 4

Alberta ranks fourth in the country for poultry production, with the average Albertan eating about 66 pounds (30 kilograms) of chicken per year, or about a pound (one-half kilogram) per week. Alberta chicken, skinless of course, has about 42% less fat than it did in 1981, a testament to its lean and healthy reputation. Chickens (*Gallus gallus domesticus*) were first domesticated from red junglefowl in Thailand around 7000 BC. They were quick to catch on as a domestic animal because they were small, inexpensive and provided a meal, either by way of the meat or the eggs. Chicken is also one of the easiest meats to digest. It pairs well with a multitude of flavours, and it is tasty on its own—the famous saying, "tastes like chicken," might not be such a bad analogy when you consider the diversity of this simple food.

2 Tbsp (30 mL) unsalted butter

1 medium yellow onion, finely chopped

2 carrots, peeled and diced

2 celery stalks, diced

1 tsp (5 mL) garlic, minced

¼ tsp (1 mL) sea salt

¼ tsp (1 mL) freshly ground black pepper

6 oz (170 gm) mushrooms, sliced

½ tsp (2 mL) fresh thyme, chopped

3 bay leaves

2 Tbsp (30 mL) dry sherry

¼ cup (60 mL) flour

2 cups (500 mL) chicken stock

1 cup cream (10%)

3 cups (750 mL) cooked chicken, cubed

½ cup (125 mL) peas, fresh or frozen

1 Tbsp (15 mL) parsley, chopped

Preheat the oven to 375° F (190° F). Butter an 8-cup (2 L) baking dish and set aside.

In a large pot, melt butter over medium-high heat and add onions, carrots and celery and cook until soft, 3 to 4 minutes. Add garlic, salt and pepper and cook, stirring, for 30 seconds. Then add mushrooms, thyme, bay leaves and cook, stirring, until the mushrooms are soft and have given off their liquid, about 3 minutes. Add sherry and cook until most of the liquid is evaporated. Stir in flour and cook, stirring, for 2 minutes. Stirring constantly, slowly add the chicken stock and cream and cook until the mixture is smooth and thickened, about 5 minutes. Add the chicken, peas and parsley, stir well, and cook until chicken is heated through. Pour filling into baking dish and set aside.

For the pastry, mix together flour, baking powder and salt in a bowl. Rub butter into the mixture until using the tips of your fingers until the mixture looks like coarse crumbs. Gently fold in buttermilk until mixture just comes together. Roll out dough on a floured surface and shape to fit the top of the baking dish.

Lay pastry on top of the filling and score pastry slightly with a knife, so it is easier to cut after baking. Brush with egg and bake for 20 to 25 minutes or until crust is golden brown.

Look for and purchase chickens that are organic, free-range animals.

Pastry

2 cups (500 mL) flour

1 Tbsp (15 mL) baking powder

1/4 tsp (1 mL) sea salt

6 Tbsp (90 mL) butter, cold

¾ cup (175 mL) buttermilk

1 egg, beaten

Pumpkin Fondue

Serves 12 as an appetizer

A diverse and warming meal that is meant to be shared, the fondue was popular in Alberta in the 1970s. Just about everyone who got married during that decade received at least one fondue pot for a wedding present. Three decades later, fondues have come back as a tasty, special part of a social gathering. You can even buy fondue pots dating from the 70s at garage sales! Fondue is certainly one of the most perfect winter foods. They can be savory or sweet, and there are many variations of the traditional cheese fondue. For example, an oil or broth can be used for meat fondues, and chocolate fondue is another popular version usually using fruit for dipping. The following pumpkin fondue is quite a departure from the traditional, but it is equally enticing.

1 sugar pumpkin, about 3 to 4 lbs (1.5 to 2 kg)

2 Tbsp (30 mL) unsalted butter

1 small onion, finely chopped

1 clove garlic, minced

1 cup (250 mL) dry white wine

pinch freshly grated nutmeg

2 Tbsp (30 mL) flour

¼ cup (60 mL) fresh sage, chopped

2 cups (500 mL) grated aged white cheddar cheese

½ cup (125 mL) sour cream

sea salt and freshly ground pepper to taste

Preheat oven to 350° F (175° C). Pierce the top of the pumpkin with a knife 3 or 4 times, and bake for 20 minutes. Let cool for 10 minutes. Remove top a quarter of the way down, forming a lid. Scoop out the seeds and fibres and set aside. Increase oven temperature to 375° F (190° C).

Melt butter in a medium saucepan and sauté onion for 5 minutes. Add garlic and cook until softened. Add white wine and bring to a simmer. Finally, add nutmeg, flour, sage and cheddar cheese and stir until the cheese is melted. Pour into the pumpkin, cover with its lid and bake for 20 minutes, until the mixture is hot. Remove from oven and stir in sour cream. Adjust salt and pepper, if needed, and serve with skewers of crusty bread for dipping and spoons for scooping out the delicious pumpkin flesh.

The word "fondue" comes from the French verb *fondre*, "to melt." Originating in the Swiss Alps, fondue was born of necessity during the winter when food was scarce. By melting hard, dry cheeses in a *caquelon* (a small, traditional earthenware pot) and enriching them with ingredients such as wine, an almost seductive meal ensued that could transform even the stalest crust of bread.

Bison Carpaccio Salad
Serves 4 to 6

Bison were the centre of life for the Native peoples of the Prairies, providing everything from nourishment, clothes and medicine to spiritual inspiration. It is commonly estimated that there were 60 million bison on the Prairies, and that the bison spread as far south as Mexico. Within just a few short years in the mid-1880s, the pressures of settlement, agriculture, drought and sport hunting drove the bison almost to extinction, thus threatening the existence of an entire way of life. Many years of hard work and dedication have saved the bison from extinction, and today we can enjoy this highly nutritious and great-tasting meat from farm-raised herds. With thick hair cover to provide protection through winter, the bison is exceptionally well suited to Alberta's climate—Alberta grows 50% of Canada's bison and 66% of Canada's organically raised bison.

1 lb (500 g) bison tenderloin

1 clove garlic, minced

2 shallots, finely diced

1 Tbsp (15 mL) balsamic vinegar

¼ cup (60 mL) extra virgin olive oil, plus additional for drizzling

2 Tbsp (30 mL) grainy Dijon mustard

¼ cup (60 mL) chopped fresh parsley

¼ cup (60 mL) chopped fresh dill

3 Tbsp (45 mL) freshly crushed peppercorns

1 bunch fresh radishes, sliced

fresh chives, thinly sliced

baby salad greens, washed and spun dry (about 2 cups [500 mL]) per person

sea salt

Combine garlic, shallots, oil and balsamic vinegar in a bowl. Place tenderloin in a pan and coat evenly with garlic mixture. Let marinate in fridge for 4 to 6 hours.

Remove tenderloin from fridge and pat dry. Season well with sea salt and peppercorns, and sear over high heat (or grill) until nicely brown, about 5 minutes. Remove from heat and let cool.

Rub mustard over entire surface of tenderloin and then roll in fresh herbs. Wrap tightly in cellophane and freeze for 3 hours to make slicing much easier.

Slice meat as thinly as possible and serve with simple greens, radishes, fresh chives, a drizzle of olive oil and a sprinkle of sea salt.

Tip
Be sure to allow yourself the 4 to 6 hours needed for the marinating and a further 3 hours for freezing. You can prepare the carpaccio ahead of time by slicing the tenderloin and laying the slices out in a circular pattern in a single layer on individual serving sized plates, covering well with cellophane and keeping in the freezer up to 5 days. Because the meat is so thinly sliced, it thaws within 5 to 10 minutes. Don't leave it longer than that because, when left too long, it loses its nice red colour.

This dish is named after Renaissance artist Vittore Carpaccio, whose work often displayed a predilection for red. Carpaccio is most often made using beef, but many foods work well in the style of carpaccio. Ultra-fresh tuna, salmon and other seafood make excellent carpaccio; just garnish with your favourite citrus. Vegetables such as zucchini—or even apple and other fruits—work well garnished with shaved cheese and toasted or candied nuts.

Apple-roasted Pheasant

Serves 4

The ring-necked pheasant *(Phasianus colchicus)* is a popular upland game bird introduced into Alberta in 1908, when 80 ring-necked pheasants were brought to the Bragg Creek area near Calgary. They have flourished ever since as a welcome addition to the Alberta landscape. Hunters bringing home pheasants have always been welcome in the kitchens of the province, and natural populations are supplemented with hatchery birds. Pheasant is available at specialty meat markets, farmers' markets and some grocery stores. Nowadays, the Canadian Pheasant Company, located in Brooks, is western Canada's largest pheasant producer, rearing about 200,000 pheasants every year. This recipe can also be made with other poultry, such as quail or chicken.

4 pheasant breasts, skin on, wing attached

sea salt and freshly cracked black pepper

1 Tbsp (15 mL) butter

1 Tbsp (15 mL) grape seed oil or olive oil

4 cups (32 oz) Pink Lady apples, peeled and sliced

¼ cup (60 mL) honey

1 Tbsp (15 mL) garlic, minced

1 tsp (5 mL) cinnamon

1 tsp (5 mL) cloves

juice of half a lemon

Preheat oven to 425° F (220° C). Season pheasant with salt and pepper. Heat butter and oil in an ovenproof sauté pan that is large enough to comfortably fit all the meat. On medium-high heat, sear pheasant breasts, skin side down, for 3 to 4 minutes until golden brown. Set aside.

Combine all the remaining ingredients in a mixing bowl and sauté in the same pan as the pheasant. When the apples are nicely caramelized, about 5 minutes, place the pheasant on top, skin sides up, and roast in the oven for 10 to 12 minutes, until the meat is cooked through.

Serve the breasts atop a spoonful of the caramelized apples.

Native to Japan and China, the pheasant is a member of the Phasianidae *family of birds, which include the quail and the peacock. Terrestrial birds that can be distinguished by the male's ornate plumage, pheasants were introduced into North America in 1881.*

Macadamia-roasted Pork with Maple Syrup

Serves 8 to 10

Pork is the fourth most important agricultural sector in Alberta after beef, wheat and canola. The province's 1500 pork producers raise 3.5 million pigs annually. In the 1950s the Lacombe, a fast-growing, high-quality meat hog, was the first breed of livestock developed in Canada—in Lacombe, of course. Pork is much lower in fat than it has ever been. To promote pork as a lean protein source, the Alberta Pork Producers have established partnerships with many of Alberta's sports teams, including the Edmonton Oilers. Domesticated some 9000 years ago, pigs are one of the earliest forms of livestock. Today, Canada produces about 30 million pigs per year and is the world's largest pork exporter—50% of our pork is exported to over 85 countries.

Stuffing

2 Tbsp (30 mL) olive oil

1 onion, finely chopped

4 cloves garlic, roughly chopped

¼ cup (60 mL) fresh rosemary, chopped

¼ cup (60 mL) fresh thyme, chopped

2 cups (500 mL) macadamia nuts, roughly chopped

¼ cup (60 mL) chicken stock

2 Tbsp (30 mL) dry bread crumbs

1 Tbsp (15 mL) dark brown sugar

2 x 3 lb (1.4 kg) pork loin rib roast, patted dry, room temperature

sea salt and freshly ground pepper

butcher twine

3–6 sprigs of fresh rosemary

1 Tbsp olive oil

Glaze

½ cup (125 mL) maple syrup

¼ cup (60 mL) white wine, preferably a Riesling

¼ cup (60 mL) chicken broth

sea salt and freshly ground pepper

Preheat oven to 400° F (200° C). Heat olive oil in a pan and cook onions, garlic, rosemary and thyme a few minutes. Add macadamia nuts. Stir in chicken stock, bread crumbs and brown sugar, and set stuffing aside.

Turn the pork loin rib roast fat side down. Slit lengthwise, almost but not quite all the way through, to form a long pocket, leaving a ½ inch (1 cm) border of uncut meat at each end. Sprinkle generously with salt and pepper. Fill the cavity with the stuffing. Tie loin together with butcher twine or heavy duty kitchen string at 1½ inch (3 to 4 cm) intervals. Slide the rosemary sprigs under the twine. Brush with remaining olive oil and sprinkle generously with salt and pepper. Set, fat side up, diagonally or curved (so it fits) on a large baking sheet or jelly roll pan.

Mix maple syrup, white wine and chicken broth together. Brush glaze mixture on meat.

Roast in the oven until a meat thermometer registers 150 to 155° F (65 to 68° C), about 2 hours, occasionally brushing with the pan drippings. Let roast rest 15 to 20 minutes out of the oven, then transfer to a carving board.

To make the sauce, stir juices around pan to loosen browned bits. Pour through a strainer into a small pan, and stir in port and chicken stock. Bring to simmer and cook until lightly thickened. Slice pork roast and serve with sauce.

Sauce

¼ cup (60 mL) port

¼ cup (60 mL) chicken stock

Duck Confit with Caramelized Rutabaga and Risotto

Serves 10

Duck hunting is a popular fall pastime in rural Alberta, but you can also buy duck at most grocery stories and specialty grocers. The world's largest mallard duck statue, with a wingspan of 25 feet (7.6 metres), is located a short drive northeast of Edmonton in the village of Andrew. Alberta also boasts its very own variety of rutabaga, "Alta Sweet," bred here by Robert Simonet. Believed to be a hybrid of a turnip and a cabbage, the rutabaga (*Brassica napus* var. *napobrassica*) has an earthy, sweet flavour and creamy flesh. Rutabagas have the extra benefit of being cancer fighters. In the recipe below, the rutabagas are caramelized to bring out their sweetness.

10 duck legs

2 heads garlic, halved crosswise

1 lemon, sliced into about 5 rings

1 orange, sliced into about 5 rings

½ cinnamon stick

4 star anise, whole

1 tsp (5 mL) black peppercorns, whole

½ inch fresh ginger, sliced into three pieces

6 sprigs of fresh thyme

3 bay leaves

½ lb (250g) kosher salt

about 2 lbs (1 kg) of rendered duck fat and 4 cups (1 L) grape seed or olive oil

Rutabaga

2 Tbsp (30 mL) butter

2 Tbsp (30 mL) brown sugar

2 small rutabaga, peeled, quartered and sliced, ¼ inch thick

sea salt and freshly ground pepper to taste

Layer the duck legs, garlic halves, lemon and orange slices, spices and herbs, in a nonreactive container, generously sprinkling with salt between each layer. Cover with plastic wrap, and cure in refrigerator for 24 hours.

Preheat the oven to 250° F (120° C). Remove the duck legs and pat them dry (you can rinse them if you prefer a milder salt flavour). Rinse and drain garlic, fruit, spices and herbs. Place duck legs and fruit mixture, alternating layers, into a deep baking dish and cover with the duck fat and oil. Bake for 6 to 8 hours or until the meat is very tender. Remove from the oven and allow the duck to cool before transferring into a crock or plastic container. Strain the fat through a fine sieve, and pour enough over the meat to cover. Once the duck legs have cooled completely, they can be stored in the refrigerator for up to three months.

To prepare the rutabaga, heat butter and brown sugar in a small pan until butter is melted. Add rutabaga slices and cook over medium heat until tender, about 12 to 15 minutes. Season with salt and pepper and set aside.

For the risotto, melt butter in a skillet over medium heat and sauté onion until softened but not coloured, about 5 minutes. Add the rice and sauté for 2 to 4 minutes, stirring to coat the grains. Then add the white wine, stir to combine until it is absorbed, about 3 minutes. Add a ladle of the hot broth, stirring slowly but continuously, until it is almost completely absorbed by the rice. Continue adding broth until all of it is absorbed and the rice is tender but slightly chewy and very creamy. This will take about 25 minutes. Stir in the remaining tablespoon of butter, parsley and Parmesan cheese. Add salt and pepper to taste. Serve the risotto piping hot with the duck confit and caramelized rutabaga.

Risotto

¼ cup (60 mL) unsalted butter, plus 1 Tbsp to finish

¼ cup (60 mL) onion, chopped

2 cups (500 mL) Arborio rice

½ cup (125 mL) white wine

5 cups hot chicken or vegetable broth

¼ cup (60 mL) parsley, chopped

½ cup (125 mL) Parmesan cheese, grated

sea salt and freshly ground pepper to taste

Chestnut and Beef Braise

Serves 6

It seems incredible, but there are more cattle in the province than there are people. Almost 772,000 tons (700,000 tonnes) of beef is produced in Alberta and a third of Alberta beef is exported to the United States. This recipe calls for a tougher cut of beef such as top side or round shoulder, which uses the technique of braising—to slowly cook the meat and vegetables (including chestnuts) in liquid to moisten and tenderize the meat. The slow cooking method helps to break down the tough fibres in the meat. The delicate texture and flavour of the chestnuts complements the beef nicely in this stew—it's hearty and melt-in-the-mouth delicious!

3 lbs (1.5 kg) inside round roast

sea salt and freshly ground pepper to taste

¼ cup (60 mL) canola or sunflower oil

1 cup (250 mL) red wine, preferably Pinot Noir

2 cups (500 mL) beef stock

1 clove garlic, crushed with a heavy knife

2 fresh Roma tomatoes, quartered

2 cups (500 mL) baby carrots

2 cups (500 mL) pearl onions

2 cups (500 mL) small white mushrooms

1 x 10 oz (283 g) jar chestnuts, drained and roughly chopped

Preheat oven to 350° F (175° C). Season meat well with salt and pepper. Heat the oil in a Dutch oven and brown the meat; remove from pan. Add red wine and bring to a rapid boil on high heat until liquid is reduced and any drippings are loosened from the bottom of the pot. Add the beef stock and stir. Return the roast to the pan and add remaining ingredients. Cover and cook in the oven until tender, about 1½ hours, turning occasionally.

Remove the meat from the pan and strain out the liquid, reserving vegetables. Reduce the sauce until thickened. Season to taste.

Place the meat on a serving dish and add reserved vegetables. Serve with the sauce and roasted potatoes.

Horse chestnut trees, although not common, are robust enough to grow in the Alberta climate, but their fruit is not edible. One horse chestnut tree in downtown Edmonton, near Jasper Avenue and 106th Street, was saved from being cut down because of its historic landscape importance in the city.

Pappardelle with Black Winter Truffles

Serves 4

Seductive and intense, French black truffles *(Tuber melanosporum)* are the world's most precious tubers. Often called "the perfume of the earth itself," the truffle is a coveted aphrodisiac, strongly scented with a musky earthiness that is evocative of sex and mystery. Truffles are related to mushrooms, but they grow underground. A pig was traditionally chosen to help sniff out the precious gems, although today the nose of a trusty dog is also used. Most truffles are harvested in late fall or winter. You can occasionally find fresh truffles at specialty markets across the province or via the Internet, but they will cost you a pretty penny—they run anywhere from $700 to $3000 dollars per pound (half kilogram). You can more easily find truffle butter, versatile truffle oil or even flash-frozen truffles, giving you the pleasure of the flavour at a reasonable cost.

Cream Sauce

- 1 Tbsp (15 mL) butter
- ¼ cup (60 mL) onion, finely chopped
- ½ cup (125 mL) white wine
- ½ cup (125 mL) heavy cream (32%)
- sea salt and freshly ground pepper
- ¼ cup (60 mL) grated Parmesan cheese

- 1 lb (500 g) fresh pappardelle, homemade (see next page) or store-bought
- 1 medium black winter truffle, grated, sliced or shaved

Melt butter in a skillet and sauté onion until soft. Add white wine and simmer until half the liquid is reduced. Stir in cream and simmer for 5 minutes. Season with salt and pepper.

Bring a large pot of salted water to a boil, add the pappardelle and cook until al dente, for about 5 minutes. Drain and transfer pasta to the skillet with the cream sauce and add Parmesan cheese. Toss gently to mix and transfer to a warm serving bowl. Grate fresh truffle over pasta and serve.

Tip

Have a pot of boiling water ready first, and you can prepare the sauce and cook the pasta at the same time.

Homemade Pasta

Mix flour and eggs on low speed in a heavy-duty electric mixer until mixture has a coarse, crumbly look, like corn meal. Add water in small quantities until the mixture starts to hold together. Switch to the dough hook on the mixer, or knead by hand 7 to 10 minutes. Dough should not be sticky or in separate pieces. Add a little more liquid if needed, or a little more flour if sticky. Cover with plastic wrap and let dough rest 15 to 30 minutes. Roll through a pasta machine according to the manufacturer's instructions.

To cook, make sure water is at a full boil and very well salted. Fresh pasta cooks very quickly and will rise to the top of the water when done. Drain in a colander and do not rinse.

1 1/2 cups (375 mL) semolina flour

2 eggs

2 to 3 tsp (10 to 15 mL) lukewarm water

Steamed Artichokes with Lemon Butter

Serves 4

Alexandra Luppold, a southern Alberta gardener known for her biodynamic lettuce and other salad greens, has added artichokes to her garden offerings, which she sells at farmers' markets and high-end restaurants in the Calgary area. Recipes calling simply for artichokes refer to the globe artichoke (*Cynara scolymus*), which was brought to North America by French and Spanish immigrants. Artichoke is a perennial thistle first cultivated in Naples in the 15th century. According to legend, Zeus fell in love with a mortal beauty named Cynara, and, when she angered him, he threw her back to earth as the thorny artichoke. In early Greek and Roman times, artichokes were considered an aphrodisiac and, because of their reputed sexual power, were reserved for consumption only by men. Much later, in 1947, the as-yet unknown Marilyn Monroe was named "Miss California Artichoke Queen"—no doubt it was a sign of things to come.

4 smallish globe artichokes

1 clove garlic, minced, finely chopped

1 bay leaf

zest and juice from 2 lemons

¼ cup (60 mL) vegetable stock

¼ cup (60 mL) white wine

½ lb (250 g) butter

Use scissors to trim the thorny tips from the artichokes and trim off top, about ⅓ inch (0.8 cm). Steam, stem end up, in a basket over water with garlic, bay leaf and lemon zest. Cook 30 to 35 minutes or until tender. Heat the vegetable stock and white wine in a medium pan and reduce to about 2 Tbsp (30 mL).

Meanwhile, cut the butter into cubes. When the stock has reduced, lower the heat and whisk the butter in 1 cube at a time until you have used all the butter and the sauce is thick. Stir in lemon juice to taste. Place the butter sauce over low heat, being careful not to let it boil. Serve the warm artichokes with the butter sauce as an appetizer.

Tip
To prevent discolouration through oxidation, sprinkle or rub the cut surfaces of artichokes with lemon juice.

Tip
Artichokes are also available canned and frozen, and you can jazz up a home-made pizza by including them as a topping.

Cauliflower and Potato Gratin

Serves 6 to 8

You don't have to go all the way to the Netherlands to get your hands on some amazing Gouda. Amazing? Try Sylvan Star Cheese—grand champion of the Dairy Farmers of Canada's Canadian Cheese Grand Prix in 2000; finalist for best artisan farmhouse cheese in 2004; and three-category champion in 2006, including best artisan farmhouse cheese and best flavoured cheese. When John and Janny Schalkwyk immigrated to Canada, they brought with them a passion for cheese and a Dutch-sized capacity for hard work. Each day starts around 4 AM with the milking of over 85 Holstein cows. Then they get to work turning and hand-waxing 700 plus cheeses. Sylvan Star Cheese produces 12,500 pounds (25,000 kilograms) of cheese each year from their farm near Red Deer. You can purchase their cheese at their small shop located right on their farm or at various farmers' markets across the province.

1½ cups (375 mL) Gruyere cheese, grated

½ cup (125 mL) Parmesan cheese, grated

1 Tbsp (15 mL) butter

1 medium onion, diced

2 cloves garlic, minced

2 cups (500 mL) heavy cream (32%)

1 tsp (5 mL) freshly grated nutmeg

4 lbs (2 kg) Yukon Gold potatoes, peeled and thinly sliced

2 medium cauliflower, sliced ¼ inch thick

sea salt and freshly ground pepper

¼ cup (60 mL) fresh thyme, chopped

Butter an 8-cup (2 L) shallow baking dish and preheat the oven to 350° F (175° C). Combine the cheeses, reserving ½ cup (125 mL) for the topping and put aside. Sauté the onions in the butter until soft, add the garlic and cook for 2 minutes. Add the cream, bring just to the boil and remove from the heat. Stir in the nutmeg. Layer the potatoes and cauliflower in the baking dish, seasoning each layer with salt and pepper and thyme and a sprinkle of the cheeses. Continue layering until you have used all the potatoes and cauliflower, and pour the cream over the vegetables. Top with the reserved cheese, cover and bake for 35 to 40 minutes or until the vegetables are tender. Remove the cover and continue cooking until the top is golden brown, about 10 more minutes. Let rest at least 10 minutes or up to ½ hour before serving.

Gratins can be made with vegetables such as zucchini, winter squash, tomatoes and leeks. They make a perfect meal together with some crusty French bread.

Roasted Jerusalem Artichokes

Serves 4

Also known as "sunchoke" and "Canada potato," the Jerusalem artichoke (*Helianthus tuberosus*) is easy to grow here and will even produce a display of small sunflowers late in the summer. In Alberta, Jerusalem artichokes are best harvested in the fall when light frosts enhance the natural sweetness. A tuber native to North America, the Jerusalem artichoke's waxy flesh has the texture of a crispy apple and the flavour reminiscent of sunflower seeds. Traditionally, the tubers were simply boiled and eaten much like potatoes, and they can be used in place of potatoes in many recipes. The first written record of this edible member of the sunflower family dates from 1603, when Samuel de Champlain encountered it growing in the vegetable gardens of First Nations peoples.

4 cloves garlic, chopped

2½ Tbsp (37 mL) extra virgin olive oil

1½ lbs (750 g) Jerusalem artichokes

sea salt and freshly ground black pepper to taste

1 Tbsp (15 mL) chopped fresh parsley

Preheat oven to 350˚ F (175˚ C). Heat garlic and oil in a small pot and cook until soft. Peel Jerusalem artichokes and cut into small chunks, placing chunks into a bowl of acidulated water (see next page) as you work. Put in a shallow roasting pan large enough to hold all in one layer comfortably. Strain garlic from oil and pour oil over the chokes. Add salt and pepper and toss.

Bake in oven for about 20 minutes, stirring one or twice, until tender. Sprinkle parsley on top and serve as a side dish.

The Jerusalem artichoke has no ties to the famous Biblical city; the name simply comes from the English misunderstanding the Italian word girasol, which means "sunflower."

Acidulated water is just water to which a little acid—normally lemon or lime juice or vinegar—has been added; ½ tsp (2 mL) per cup (250 mL) is enough. When you are peeling or cutting fruits or vegetables that discolour quickly when exposed to air, like apples, place them in acidulated water to prevent browning. Jerusalem artichokes, globe artichokes and salsify are just some of the foods that benefit from this treatment. Acidulated water is also sometimes used for cooking.

Pancetta and Pine Nut Brussels Sprouts

Serves 6

Because it does well in cool climates, Brussels sprouts (*Brassica oleracea* var. *gemmifera*) are perfectly suited to Alberta; they even improve in flavour, sweetness and tenderness if allowed to chill through a few frosts. Brussels sprouts came originally from the region around Afghanistan and, like cauliflower, is actually a variety of cabbage. The vegetable was reputedly first cultivated in large quantities in Belgium, hence its name. Because Brussels sprouts are often overcooked, they do not hold a place among the stars of vegetable kingdom. Overcooking releases the sprouts' naturally occurring sulfur, giving them a pungent smell and taste. When properly cooked—especially if given an opportunity to "ripen" during a frost—this vegetable is sweet and nutty, and it provides many nutritional benefits, such as vitamins C and D, folic acid and dietary fibre.

2 lbs (1 kg) Brussels sprouts

splash of olive oil

5 oz (140 g) pancetta, diced

sea salt and freshly ground pepper to taste

½ cup (125 mL) pine nuts, toasted

Preheat oven to 400° F (200° C). Slice the Brussels sprouts in half lengthwise, removing any loose, outer leaves and trimming the bottom stems. Toss in olive oil and add pancetta, season with salt and pepper. Spread in a single layer on a baking sheet. Stir occasionally, so the Brussels sprouts cook evenly.

Bake for 20 to 30 minutes, until pancetta is crispy. Toss with the pine nuts and another splash of olive oil, if desired.

Tip
To toast pine nuts, place in a dry frying pan and cook on low heat, stirring occasionally until lightly golden.

Pancetta is Italian bacon, which is available at most delis and Italian markets.

Maple Candied Sweet Potatoes

Serves 4 to 6

Another indigenous tuber, the sweet potato *(Ipomoea batatas)* is a traditional Alberta accompaniment to Thanksgiving dinner. Probably dating back to Peru as early as 8000 BC, the sweet potato is often confused with the yam, a vegetable native to West Africa. A member of the magnolia family, the sweet potato is only distantly related to the potato. Although not commonly eaten, the leaves and shoots of the sweet potato plant are also edible and make an interesting addition to salads. The most popular sweet potato varieties in Alberta are "Garnet" and "Jewel," which do well in our northern climate. They are extra sweet and have striking orange flesh.

1 cup (250 mL) maple syrup

1 cup (250 mL) orange juice

½ cup (125 mL) fresh lime juice

½ cup (125 mL) water

¼ cup (60 mL) melted butter

3 lbs (1.5 kg) sweet potatoes

Combine maple syrup, fruit juices and water in a nonreactive saucepan large enough to hold all the sweet potatoes comfortably. Bring to a boil, then reduce to a simmer.

Peel the sweet potatoes, slicing the longer ones in half, and place in the saucepan. Cook, turning occasionally, for about one and a half hours, or until the edges of the sweet potatoes turn slightly translucent and they are tender.

Transfer onto a serving platter and drizzle with the melted butter.

Ipomoea batatas is vigorous, twining, climbing annual vine that is grown in containers for its attractive foliage rather than its flowers.

Creamy Espresso Martini

Serves 1

Two-thirds of Albertans drink coffee every day, and its caffeine content and flavour have made coffee the second most popular beverage choice after water. Coffee (*Coffea* species) was discovered in Ethiopia—legend has it by a farmer who noticed his goat's boisterous behaviour after eating some berries. Only when the berries (they are actually seeds, not beans) reached Turkey in the 15th century were they roasted and crushed to make an early version of today's beverage. The coffee industry today employs an astounding 20 million people and is second in value only to petroleum products in international trade.

1 oz (30 mL) cold espresso

1½ oz (45 mL) vodka, coffee or vanilla flavour

1½ oz (45 mL) coffee liqueur

1 oz (30 mL) Irish cream liqueur

1 scoop (¼ cup [60 mL]) vanilla ice cream

Pour ingredients into a shaker and shake vigorously, and strain into a chilled martini glass.

Did you know that most people employed to grow and harvest coffee beans live well below the poverty line and receive little income for their labour? To help you enjoy your java guilt-free, we recommend you seek out and purchase Fair Trade organically grown coffee.

Caramel-dipped Apples

Serves 8

In Alberta, you can pick fresh apples every year at U-pick farms. For example, Sprout Farms in Bon Accord, a nursery that recently became a U-pick destination, boasts over 25 years of fruit-growing experience in the province. In the 1920s, hardy apples were first being promoted on the Prairies as a tree fruit option, but it wasn't until the 1970s that tasty and very hardy varieties such as the Norland became popular here. Many of these hardy apples were developed at the Agriculture Canada Research Centre in Morden, Manitoba. Today, apples have the honour of being Canada's number one fruit crop, with over 454,000 tons (412,000 tonnes) grown every year.

1 lb (500 g) dark brown sugar

¾ cup (175 mL) unsalted butter, room temperature

1 x 10 oz (300 mL) can sweetened condensed milk

⅔ cup (150 mL) light corn syrup

1/4 tsp (1 mL) sea salt

1 tsp (5 mL) vanilla

¼ cup (60 mL) whipping cream

8 firm apples, such as Granny Smith, stems removed, washed and dried

8 wooden sticks such as craft sticks, popsicle sticks or even chopsticks

Combine brown sugar, butter, condensed milk, corn syrup and salt in a heavy-bottomed pot over medium-low heat and stir slowly but continually to dissolve sugar until it reaches a temperature between 234° F and 240° F (112° C and 115° C) on a candy thermometer, or the soft-ball stage (see opposite). Remove from heat, stir in vanilla and whipping cream and pour into a clean metal bowl. Cool until caramel is 200° F (95° C), about 15 minutes.

While caramel is cooling, line a baking sheet with buttered parchment paper and push one stick into the stem end of each apple. Dip apples in caramel and let excess caramel drip off before setting on the greased paper. Cool before eating and chill any uneaten apples, wrapped in cellophane, up to one week.

Tip

If your apples are quite waxy, dip them in boiling water for 30 seconds to remove the wax and dry very well.

Tip

Once the caramel apples have set, dip them into melted chocolate for an extra decadent Halloween treat. You can also roll them in chopped nuts, candy sprinkles or crushed candy bars!

Tip
The soft-ball stage is a candy test where you drop a little syrup in cold water, and as the syrup cools, it forms a soft ball that flattens when it is removed from the water.

Cucumber and Fresh Dill Salad

Serves 6

Cucumbers are harvested in southern Alberta greenhouses from around the beginning of February, followed by the rest of the province later in the month. The cucumber (*Cucumis sativa*) was first cultivated in India over 3000 years ago. Cucumbers are members of the squash family, which, along with corn and beans, formed the "Three Sisters" of early Native American cuisine. In 1535 Jacques Cartier found "very great cucumbers" growing in what is now Montréal. Because cucumbers are 95% water, they are not especially nutritionally dense, but they are a good source of vitamins C and K, silica and potassium. This water-rich refreshing fruit can also be enjoyed in the heat of summer to keep you feeling as "cool as a cucumber." Fresh dill is available year-round in most supermarkets. For summer use, you can easily grow both dill and cucumbers in your garden.

4 large, long English cucumbers

1 medium red onion, halved and thinly sliced

1 bunch fresh dill, finely chopped, about 1 cup (250 mL)

¼ cup (60 mL) cider vinegar

1–2 Tbsp (15–30 mL) honey, to taste

1 cup (250 ml) sour cream or plain yogurt

sea salt and freshly ground pepper to taste

Wash the cucumbers and peel in lengthwise strips, being sure to leave a bit of dark green skin between each strip. Thinly slice, and place slices, along with the onion and fresh dill, in a large glass bowl.

In a separate, small bowl, make a dressing with the vinegar, honey, sour cream and salt and pepper. Add dressing to large bowl and mix well to combine.

Allow the salad to sit for at least 15 minutes before serving as a side dish.

Although considered a vegetable, cucumbers are actually the fruit of the cucumber plant, which belongs to the same family of plants as melons and pumpkins.

Mixed Citrus Salad with Lemongrass Vinaigrette

Serves 4

Oranges, lemons and limes originated as wild fruit in Southeast Asia thousands of years ago. Their taste, colour and fragrance made them very popular, and many cultures contributed to their spread across the globe. Today, citrus fruits are cultivated in about 140 countries, with about half of the total production dedicated to oranges. Citrus fruits are particularly popular and much appreciated in winter because of their long storage qualities and refreshingly bright taste. And we can't forget the long-anticipated Christmas oranges (mandarins, clementines, satsumas), with their easy-to-peel skin and super sweet taste. They have surely become as much a part of an Alberta Christmas as snow and St. Nick.

2 large grapefruit, peeled, and segmented

2 oranges, peeled and segmented

2 blood oranges, peeled and segmented

½ cup (125 mL) kumquats, sliced in thin rounds

1 star fruit, sliced crosswise

handful of fresh mint, chopped

Dressing

1 stalk lemongrass, tender bottom only

½ cup (125 mL) apple juice

2 Tbsp (30 mL) honey or agave syrup

1 Tbsp (15 mL) shallots, finely chopped

zest and juice from 1 lime

2 Tbsp (30 mL) canola or sunflower oil

Combine the fruit in a medium-sized bowl and let sit for 15 minutes.

For the dressing, bruise and roughly chop the lemongrass. In a small saucepan, combine apple juice, honey or agave juice, lemongrass and bring to a boil and cook for 5 minutes. Remove saucepan from heat and let cool to room temperature. Add shallots, lime zest and juice and oil, and whisk together until well blended.

Toss citrus fruit and mint with dressing and serve.

Oranges were not named for their colour—the word "orange" comes from the Sanskrit naranga, *which means "fragrant." Scurvy, a condition resulting from vitamin C deficiency, was a major problem throughout the exploration and settlement of Canada. It could be prevented or cured by eating citrus fruit such as oranges.*

Potato and Roasted Garlic Chowder

Serves 4

The first potatoes to grow in Alberta were from seed potatoes the early settlers brought from their homelands in the 1880s. By 1917 a collaboration of 15 growers planted the first commercial potato crop on 300 acres (120 hectares) in the Lethbridge area. Less than 10% of the over 90 varieties of Alberta potatoes go to market fresh. The rest are processed for French fries, potato chips, etc., or used for seed potatoes. Because of our cool climate, which produces potatoes with few diseases and pest problems, Alberta is the country's number one exporter of seed potatoes.

2 medium onions, diced

¼ cup (60 mL) unsalted butter

1 Tbsp (15 mL) olive oil

2 cups (500 mL) celery, diced

1 cup (250 mL) carrots, diced

4 medium potatoes, peeled and diced

1 bay leaf

vegetable or chicken stock, enough to just cover vegetables

2 bulbs roasted garlic (see next page), cloves squeezed out and roughly chopped

2 cups (500 ml) heavy cream (32%)

sea salt and freshly ground pepper to taste

¼ cup (60 ml) fresh herbs such as parsley, thyme or mint, chopped

In a heavy pot, sauté the onions in the butter and oil until they turn golden. Add the vegetables, bay leaf and cover with stock. Simmer for 15 minutes, then add the roasted garlic and cream, and simmer for 10 to 15 minutes more or until the potatoes are cooked and the soup is reduced and creamy. Season to taste with salt and pepper. Ladle soup into bowls and garnish with a sprinkle of herbs.

Roasted Garlic

You can roast as little or as much garlic as you want. I tend to roast 5 or 6 bulbs at a time, so I will have leftovers to last a week. Preheat the oven to 350° F (175° C). Slice the top of each bulb of garlic to expose the cloves, and lay them cut side up in a baking dish. Drizzle with olive oil and sprinkle with sea salt. Roast 20 to 30 minutes or until cloves are tender. Remove from oven and set aside until cool enough to handle. The buttery flesh of the cloves will come out of the bulb easily when you squeeze it (throw out the papery skin of the bulb). Alternatively, you can serve the whole roasted bulbs as a garnish to grilled meats or vegetables.

Warthog Ale and Cheddar Soup

Serves 4

Ed McNally owns the province's most recognizable microbrewery, Big Rock Brewery, named after the huge glacial erratic in a field southwest of Okotoks. After a successful career as a lawyer, Ed began farming barley and quickly became interested in brewing beer, a childhood dream for the Lethbridge-born entrepreneur. Big Rock Brewery came to be in 1984, but it wasn't until the summer of 1986—and a strike at the big corporate breweries—that Big Rock really sank its teeth into the Alberta terrain. All of a sudden, the brewery had to schedule its dedicated employees in shifts around the clock to keep up with the demand for what was the only beer available during that hot summer. Today, nary a beer-drinking Albertan hasn't enjoyed one of the eight (soon to be nine) varieties of über-quality ales that are available anywhere thirst-quenching beverages are sold.

2 medium onions, diced

1 Tbsp (15 ml) olive oil

¼ cup (60 ml) unsalted butter

2 cups (500 ml) celery, diced

1 cup (250 ml) parsnips, diced

4 medium potatoes, peeled and diced

1 bay leaf

vegetable or chicken stock, enough to just cover vegetables

2 cups (500 ml) heavy cream (32%)

2 cups sharp white Cheddar cheese, grated

½ to 1 bottle of Warthog Ale, about 6 to 12 oz (170 to 341 mL) or to taste

sea salt and freshly ground pepper

In a heavy pot, sauté the onions in the butter and oil until they turn golden. Add celery, parsnips, potatoes, bay leaf and add enough stock to cover everything. Simmer for 15 minutes, then add the cream and simmer for 10 to 15 minutes more or until the potatoes are cooked and the soup is reduced and creamy. Remove soup from heat and blend in cheese in small batches. Return to medium-low heat and stir in ale to taste. Season with salt and pepper and serve.

The Okotoks erratic is a huge chunk of rock weighing 16,500 tons (16,700 tonnes) brought from Jasper National Park to its current destination by the flow of glacial ice 10,000 years ago. The Big Rock, which figures in Blackfoot stories, is a famous landmark that is impossible to overlook.

Hearty Lentil Soup

Serves 4 to 6

Lentils are pulses or legumes, a group of plants where the seed is grown in a pod; for example, chickpeas and beans. Very high in protein and essential amino acids and endowed with a long storage life, lentils are an important crop worldwide. Canada is the world's largest exporter of lentils, with the majority of lentils imported by India. Saskatchewan produces the bulk of Canada's lentils, with Alberta taking second place. Over 10,000 acres (4000 hectares) of land is dedicated to lentil production in Alberta every year. Lentils should be a staple in every pantry; they cook quickly, are delicious in salads and soups and can be used as a meat substitute in many dishes, such as meat loaf and burgers.

½ tsp (2 mL) cinnamon

¼ tsp (1 mL) cloves

1 Tbsp (15 mL) cumin

2 tsp (10 mL) olive oil

1 cup (250 mL) onions, chopped

1 clove garlic, minced

½ cup (125 mL) carrot, diced

1 large bay leaf

½ inch (1 cm) piece fresh ginger, peeled and chopped

2 cups (500 mL) dried red lentils, rinsed

water

1 Tbsp (15 mL) apple cider vinegar

2 tsp (10 mL) cilantro, chopped

salt and freshly ground pepper to taste

finely sliced chives for garnish

In a small pan, toast the cinnamon, cloves and cumin until very fragrant, about 1 to 2 minutes. Set aside.

In a medium-sized pot, heat oil over medium-high heat and sauté onions until translucent. Add garlic, carrots, bay leaf, ginger with the toasted cinnamon, cloves and cumin and sauté about 2 minutes. Add lentils and add enough water to cover by 1 inch (2.5 cm) and cook 30 to 45 minutes, or until the lentils are completely soft. Stir in the apple cider vinegar and cilantro. Season with salt and plenty of pepper. Garnish each serving with chives.

Distinctly Albertan is the best way to describe Joe St. Denis's peabutter. No, that's not a typo. A veteran pea farmer of 20 years on his Legal farm north of Edmonton, St. Denis came up with the idea to produce an allergy-free alternative to peanut butter. Peanuts are Canada's number one allergy-producing food, creating reactions that are often so severe that many schools have banned its inclusion in children's lunch boxes. Thanks to St. Denis and his "NoNuts Peabutter," which not only looks but also tastes like the real thing, everyone can enjoy peabutter and jelly sandwiches without fear.

Alberta Stew

Serves 6

Synonymous with winter and cold, a stew is simply thick soup with chunky cuts of vegetables, meat or seafood—or a combination thereof. Offering a hearty and frugal meal that keeps for many days, stews freeze well and can be made in quantities to feed many, all in the convenience of one pot. In Alberta, many popular stews such as goulash, gumbo and Irish stew enjoy long culinary histories. The stew given here is made from homegrown ingredients: the village of Mundare is home of the famous Stawnichy's kielbassa, a Ukrainian-style sausage for which the town is best known. In 1959 Woytko Stawnichy started his sausage business with one smokehouse, and the business has since won numerous awards for its superior products.

1 to 2 Tbsp (15 to 30 mL) canola oil

¾ lb (375 g) Mundare sausage, cut into ¼ inch (.5 cm) slices

1 yellow onion, diced

2 medium carrots, peeled and sliced diagonally

2 celery stalks, sliced diagonally

½ cup (125 mL) dry white wine

6 cloves garlic, finely chopped

¾ lb (375 mL) venison, cut into 1 inch (2.5 cm) pieces

1 x 19 oz (540 mL) can crushed tomatoes

4 cups (1 L) vegetable stock

2 Tbsp (30 mL) fresh thyme or 1 tsp (5 mL) dried thyme

¼ cup (60 mL) fresh parsley, chopped

1 tsp (5 mL) salt

pinch of chipotle powder or cayenne

freshly ground pepper

In a large pot, heat the oil over moderately high heat. Add Mundare sausage and cook, stirring frequently, until lightly browned and heated through, about 5 minutes.

Add onion and cook, stirring occasionally, about 5 minutes, then add the carrots and celery and cook for another 5 minutes. Add the white wine and garlic, bring to a simmer, and cook until reduced to about ¼ cup (60 mL), about 3 minutes. Add venison, tomatoes, vegetable stock, thyme, parsley, salt and chipotle powder. Cover, bring to a simmer and cook for 20 minutes. Add freshly ground pepper, and taste and adjust seasoning, if necessary.

Tip
Bison can be used in place of the venison.

To recognize the contribution to the community by the Stawnichys, a 42-foot (12.8-metre) high, 6-ton (7-tonne) statue of their famous kielbassa was erected in 2001, and it has become a popular Alberta roadside attraction.

Caramelized Onion and Goat Cheese Tart

Serves 6

Because they are such great keepers, onions (*Allium cepa*) are a perfect winter food. They are also extremely versatile and lend themselves to many uses. They can be eaten raw or cooked, chopped or whole. Introduced to North America by Columbus in 1493, they have been a prized food for thousands of years—they were often presented as gifts or even used as payment for goods or lodging. A naturally occurring antioxidant, quercetin, contributes to the reputation onions have for being healthy. Onions grow well in our climate, and Alberta is home to the wild white onion (*A. textile*), known for its combined garlic and onion flavour.

1 Tbsp (15 mL) oil

1 Tbsp (15 mL butter

6 medium yellow onions, thinly sliced

sea salt to taste

1 tsp (5 mL) sugar

1 Tbsp (15 mL) balsamic vinegar

Béchamel

2 Tbsp (30 mL) butter

2 Tbsp (30 mL) flour

1 cup (250 mL) milk

1 bay leaf

pinch of nutmeg

1 x ¾ lb (397 g) package frozen puff pastry, thawed

egg wash made with 1 beaten egg and a splash of water

8 oz (250 g) goat cheese

2 Tbsp chopped fresh herbs, such as parsley, thyme or sage (optional)

Heat oil and butter in a large pan over medium heat. Add the onions, season with salt and cook until softened, about 6 minutes. Stir in the sugar and balsamic vinegar, turn the heat to medium low and cook for 30 to 45 minutes, stirring often, until nicely caramelized.

To make the béchamel, melt the butter in a small, heavy saucepan over low heat. Add flour into melted butter and stir over low heat for 5 to 7 minutes. Slowly add milk, bay leaf and nutmeg, stirring constantly, and cook for about 10 more minutes until smooth and thick.

Preheat oven to 400° F (200° C). Roll out the pastry to ⅛ inch (.25 cm) thick and place on a rectangular baking sheet. Prick all over with a fork. Brush the outside edges, about ½ inch (1 cm) with egg wash.

Combine onions and béchamel sauce in a bowl. Crumble in goat cheese and fresh herbs, if desired, and stir to combine.

Spread onion mixture onto pastry and bake for 15 to 20 minutes until pastry is puffed and golden. Let sit 10 minutes before cutting into squares. Serve warm or at room temperature with a lightly dressed green salad and port sauce (recipe opposite).

In a small saucepan, combine port and stock and reduce over medium heat until thick and syrupy.

Tip
This tart is perfect for picnics, potlucks and lazy Sunday brunches. Best served at room temperature or slightly warm, it makes a great "do ahead" choice for travelling or entertaining. It also could be done in individual tart shells for easy serving.

Port Sauce
1 cup (250 mL) port
½ cup (125 mL) chicken stock

Eggplant "Haggis"

Serves 6 to 8

Fair fa' your honest, sonsie face,
Great chieftain o' the puddin'-race!

Definitely a case of love it or leave it, haggis is the national dish of Scotland, the country that provided many immigrants to Alberta in the early 1900s. Traditional haggis is a mixture of sheep organs and oatmeal stuffed into a sheep's stomach, which is then boiled and served like a big sausage. It is presented with *neeps* and *tatties* (turnips and potatoes, although the turnips are what we know today as ruta-bagas). The much-loved Scottish poet Robert Burns (1759–96) wrote the poem *Address to a Haggis*, and he is credited with making the dish famous worldwide. Each year on January 25, many people in Alberta commemorate Burns' birthday with a reading of the poem accompanying the elaborate carving and serving of the dish. Here is a vegetarian alternative to make for Robbie Burns' day.

1 large eggplant

1 cup (250 mL) red lentils

½ tsp (2 mL) sea salt

2 cups (500 mL) water

1 Tbsp (15 mL) tomato paste

dash of hot red pepper sauce

⅓ cup (75 mL) fine grain bulgur

1 large onion, finely chopped

splash of olive oil

1 clove garlic, minced

pinch each of cumin and coriander

1 to 2 Tbsp (15 to 30 mL) fresh parsley and mint, chopped

sea salt and freshly ground pepper to taste

Preheat oven to 350° F (175° C). Bake eggplant for 15 minutes or until starting to soften. Allow to cool to room temperature then cut the top end off and, using a small knife, loosen the flesh around the inside of the eggplant. Scoop out the remaining flesh, being careful not to tear the skin. Set aside the skin for the filling. (You can save the eggplant flesh for another recipe.)

Bring lentils and salted water to a boil over high heat. Turn the heat to low and simmer until the lentils are yellow and very mushy, 20 to 30 minutes, skimming off the foam that collects on the surface as they cook. Stir in tomato paste and hot red pepper sauce to taste.

Put bulgur into a bowl and pour the hot lentil mixture over it. Stir well, cover and set aside for half an hour.

Robbie might roll over in his grave at the sight and taste of an eggplant haggis, but he no doubt would be pleased that his words have stood the test of time.

Meanwhile, in a skillet sauté onion in olive oil in medium-high heat until it starts to caramelize. Add garlic, cumin, coriander and plenty of freshly ground pepper. Cook about 2 minutes more. Set aside.

Allow the bulgur and lentil mixture to sit for 30 minutes and then add the onion mixture and mix everything together very well. Add the fresh parsley and mint and season with salt and pepper, if needed.

Stuff lentil mixture into eggplant shell and place in an oiled baking dish. Bake at 350° F (175° C) for 20 to 30 minutes, until hot all the way through. Slice and serve.

Cabbage Rolls

Serves 4

Cooks love to make little packages of food for their families, and cabbage leaves lend themselves particularly well to this task. Because cabbage rolls appear in so many cuisines, spanning continents, languages and centuries, it is difficult to pin down their origin. Large numbers of Ukrainian settlers came to settle in what is now Alberta beginning in the early 1890s, bringing their version of stuffed cabbage rolls, Borscht and pierogi. Many Albertans have fond memories of a kitchen full of women—from multiple generations of family—making dozens and dozens of delicious cabbage rolls for an upcoming holiday meal or feast at a special gathering.

1½ cups (375 mL) rice

2 cups (500 mL) vegetable or chicken stock for rice AND 2 cups or more stock for cooking cabbage rolls

1 large onion, diced

2 cloves garlic, minced

¼ cup (60 mL) butter

1 lb (500 g) fresh brown mushrooms, sliced

¼ cup (60 mL) fresh thyme, chopped

sea salt and freshly ground pepper to taste

1 medium head cabbage

2 cups (500 mL) tomato sauce

¼ cup (60 mL) heavy cream (32%)

Put rice in a pot with 2 cups (500 mL) vegetable or chicken stock. Bring to a boil, cover and simmer 10 minutes. Let sit off heat 10 minutes.

Sauté onion and garlic in butter in a pan. Add mushrooms and cook until liquid has evaporated. Stir in thyme. Add salt and pepper, and adjust to taste.

In a large bowl, combine this filling mixture with the rice. Set aside.

Cut out core from the cabbage. Bring a large pot of water to a boil and cook cabbage, pulling off leaves as they soften. Drain leaves in a colander or on paper towels. Trim tough stems from cabbage

Other small packets of food from various cuisines now popular in Alberta include dolmades and spanikopita (Greek), samosas (Indian), calzones (Italian), cornish pasties (Scottish) spring rolls and wontons (Asian).

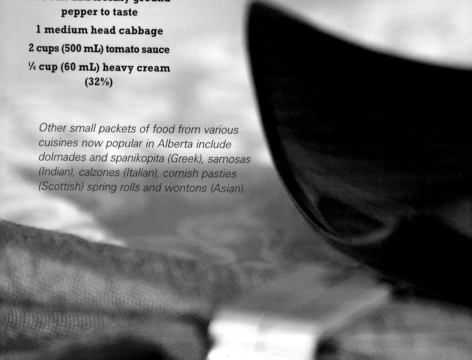

leaves and lay the leaves flat on a work surface. Place ½ cup (125 mL) filling at base of each leaf, beginning at the thick end of the leaf. Begin rolling at this end, folding edges in as you go to make a neat roll. Place finished cabbage rolls in a casserole dish and cover tightly. Recipe can be completed to this stage up to 24 hours in advance.

Heat tomato sauce in a saucepan. Bring to a boil and add cream. Simmer for 5 minutes and adjust seasoning, if needed.

Preheat oven to 375° F (190° C). Heat the vegetable or chicken stock and pour the hot stock over cabbage rolls just enough to cover them. Bake covered for 25 to 30 minutes until heated through.

Serve with hot tomato sauce and cucumber dill salad.

Roasted Turkey

Serves 8 to 10

Merriam's Turkey *(Meleagris gallopavo merriami)* is the subspecies of wild turkey native to southern Alberta. Farm-raised Merriam's Turkey is available through First Nature Farms, located in Peace River County. The Kitts family owns and operates this fully certified organic farm, which is known for its superior quality products and standards; they sell their wares at farmers' markets and specialty stores in Grande Prairie, Edmonton and Calgary. In addition to wild turkey, the Kitts family produces several other kinds of organic meat, including bison and pork, and they even make an all-natural pet food. Turkeys were domesticated by the Mayans and remain a staple ingredient in Mexican cuisine, most famously as the starring ingredient in a traditional *mole*. Wild turkeys, which differ from domesticated turkeys in that they are smaller in size and agile flyers, range from Central America to southern Canada, where they are a popular game bird.

1 x 12 lb (6 kg) turkey, fresh or thawed completely, if frozen

sea salt and freshly ground pepper

1 to 2 cups (250 to 500 mL) water or chicken broth (optional)

Preheat oven to 450° F (230° C). Set turkey out at room temperature for 45 minutes. Remove neck, giblets and any fat from cavity. Rinse turkey, pat dry with paper towels and season well with lots of salt and pepper. Place in a roasting pan and roast for 1¾ to 2 hours, or until an instant-read thermometer inserted into the thickest part of the thigh reads 170° F (77° C) and the juices run clear. Check the turkey after 1 hour, and if drippings are becoming too dark, add 1 to 2 cups of water or chicken broth into the pan. Remove the roasted turkey from the oven and let it rest for at least 20 minutes before carving.

Tip
Roasted turkey is a tried-
and-true traditional dish
for the holiday season.
Try it with side dishes
like Pancetta and Pine Nut
Brussels Sprouts (p. 112),
Maple Candied Sweet
Potatoes (p. 114), Cauliflower
and Potato Gratin (p. 108) or
Balsamic-glazed Root Vegetables
(p. 146).

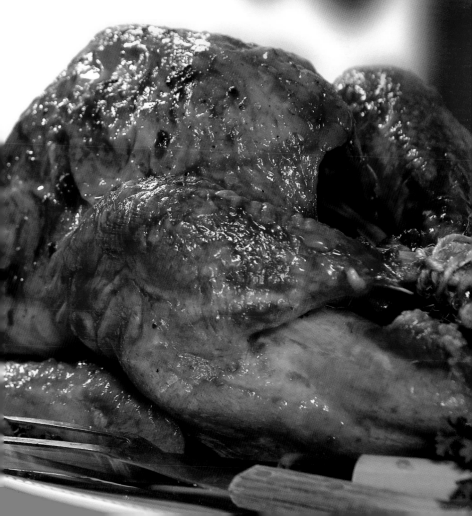

White Wine and Garlic Mussels

Serves 4 to 6

Albertans can enjoy fresh East Coast mussels throughout most of the year, but the winter months produce the sweetest mussel flesh. Long enjoyed by coastal First Nations peoples of Canada, mussels have been actively cultivated since the 1970s to meet steadily growing consumer demand. In 2003 nearly 23,000 tons (21,000 tonnes) of mussels were harvested. Mussels require a great deal of care to cultivate, and they take between 18 months and two years to mature. The mussel larvae are collected from the wild and then suspended on long lines in bays along the East Coast. Plenty of fresh water and food contributes to some of the tastiest mussels available.

4 lbs (2 kg) mussels

1 cup (250 mL) white wine such as Chardonnay

Scrub mussels under cool running water and remove any beards. Discard mussels that don't close when gently tapped.

4 garlic cloves, minced

1 Tbsp (15 mL) butter

¼ cup (60 mL) chives, chopped

Place white wine and garlic in a large pot and bring to a boil. Add mussels to the pot, cover and reduce heat, cooking for about 5 to 6 minutes. Discard any mussels that have not opened. With a slotted spoon transfer the mussels into serving dishes.

Turn heat to high and bring the remaining liquid to a boil. Cook for 2 to 3 minutes, until it has reduced slightly, and whisk in butter. Spoon the sauce over mussels, sprinkle with chives and serve hot.

Tip

Use your fresh mussels within 24 hours of purchasing them. The best way to store fresh mussels is to put them in a colander and place the colander into a bowl. Cover the mussels with ice and then with a damp towel. The mussels will stay very cold and have good air circulation, without being submerged (or drowned) in water.

Citrus Perch

Serves 4

Perch *(Perca flavescens)* are found in lakes and rivers throughout Alberta, and they are the number one sport fish in the province. The first recorded sighting of this native fish in Alberta was in 1919, in both Pine Lake and Sylvan Lake. Adult perch weigh in at around a pound (half a kilogram), and they are most popular during ice-fishing season because, unlike many other fish, they feed year-round. Alberta offers a multitude of fishing guides who know exactly where to go for your next search for this popular fish.

3 to 4 lb (1.5 to 2 kg)
fresh lake perch,
gutted and filleted

1 orange

1 lemon

1 lime

2 Tbsp (30 mL) butter

sea salt and freshly
ground pepper

Preheat grill to 450° F (230° C). Thinly slice the lemon, orange and lime. Layer fish, citrus fruit and butter on the aluminum foil, seasoning each layer with salt and pepper. Wrap the foil around fish, making sure it is well sealed, and cook for 7 to 10 minutes.

Tip
This versatile recipe can also be used to cook fresh fish over the campfire. Try it with your favourite catch-of-the-day.

Tempura

Although indulging in fried food is always tempting, it seems especially so in our Alberta winters. And if you are going to break your diet, better to do it at home where at least you can use fresh, good quality oil and ingredients. Batter-laced deep-frying is a method of cooking that was introduced to Japan by Portuguese missionaries during the 16th century. By the 17th century, Tokyo street vendors were selling tempura, using fish freshly caught in Tokyo Bay and most often fried in sesame oil. The word *tempura* comes from the Latin *ad tempora cuaresmae*, meaning "in the time of Lent"—as good Catholics, the Portuguese missionaries substituted fish for meat at this time of the year, and batter-frying was a popular presentation.

peanut oil

1 egg, beaten

1 cup (250 mL) cold beer

2 Tbsp (30 mL) dry white wine

½ cup (125 mL) flour

¼ cup (60 mL) rice flour

¼ cup (60 mL) corn starch

variety of vegetables and seafood, cut into bite-sized pieces

Heat peanut oil in a pan or deep fryer until temperature is 375° F (190° C). Combine egg, beer and white wine in a small bowl. In another bowl, combine flour, rice flour and cornstarch. Add liquid to dry mixture and very lightly mix together. The batter should look lumpy. Dip vegetables and seafood in tempura batter and fry in small batches until golden and crispy.

Tip
Keys to tasty, crispy tempura are a very light mixing of the batter—lumps are GOOD—and using an ice cold liquid, preferably one that is carbonated. To avoid greasy, soggy tempura, it is important to maintain the proper temperature of the oil, so it's best to have a thermometer on hand.

Tip
For deep-frying, peanut oil should be 2 to 3 inches (5 to 7.5 cm) deep in pot or use deep fryer according to the manufacturer's directions.

Traditionally, the Japanese mix their tempura batter with chopsticks, ensuring that it is never overmixed.

Balsamic-glazed Root Vegetables

Serves 4

Because of their excellent keeping qualities, root vegetables are important as winter food. The term "root vegetable" is a general collective term that has come to include all vegetables, from a variety of families, that grow underground; for example, potatoes, carrots, onions, rutabagas and beets. Root vegetables, an important food source for Alberta's early settlers, provided vital nourishment for families through the long winters. These vegetables were easy to grow, lasted months on the shelf, and were filling and carbohydrate-dense. Even today, when many exotic imported vegetables are available in winter in Alberta's grocery stores, root vegetables remain staples through winter for the same reasons they benefited our ancestors.

Root vegetables

1 lb (500 g) baby potatoes, a variety if possible, washed and halved or quartered, depending on size

2 medium parsnips, peeled and quartered lengthwise, then halved

1 medium yam, halved then sliced ¼ inch thick

1 small beet, washed and quartered with skin on

1 large carrot, peeled and quartered lengthwise, then halved

1 bulb garlic, broken into cloves, peeled and left whole

1 small yellow onion, peeled and quartered

Marinade

¼ cup (60 mL) balsamic vinegar

¼ cup (60 mL) extra virgin olive oil or melted butter

2 Tbsp (30 mL) honey

¼ cup (60 mL) fresh parsley, finely chopped

sea salt and freshly ground pepper to taste

2 sprigs fresh thyme

2 sprigs fresh rosemary

Preheat oven to 375° F (190° C). Combine first four ingredients of the marinade and set aside.

Place the vegetables into a large mixing bowl. Pour the prepared marinade over top, season with salt and pepper and toss to coat. Place into 13 x 9-inch (33 x 23 cm) pan and assemble the rosemary and thyme sprigs on top. Roast uncovered, turning once or twice, for about 45 minutes or until the edges are golden brown and when pierced easily with a knife. Toss with fresh parsley and serve as a side dish.

Balsamic vinegar is an aged reduction sauce that originates from Modena, Italy. The best balsamic vinegar is aged a long time, comes in very small bottles and is very expensive. Instead, try a cheaper variety but not the cheapest—it's most likely just red vinegar with brown sugar or caramel.

Brandied Seville Marmalade with Lemon and Ginger

Makes 4 x 1 cup (250 mL) jars

In Alberta, you will find Seville oranges in your local grocery stores as early as late December through to February, also an ideal time for making jams and marmalades and lifting your spirits during these cold winter months. Closely related to the Bergamot orange, which is used to flavour Earl Grey tea, the Seville orange is a species of bitter orange (*Citrus aurantium*) that originated in Vietnam. Inedible fresh, the Seville orange is prized for making marmalades, compotes and liqueurs, and is the traditional ingredient in duck a l'orange. Because it was the Spaniards who first introduced this orange to the New World, it became associated with the famous Spanish city of Seville, where many of the streets are lined with Seville orange trees.

2 lbs (1 kg) Seville oranges (about 6) halved crosswise

2 lemons, halved crosswise

⅔ cup (150 mL) candied ginger, thinly sliced

water

sugar

⅓ cup (75 mL) brandy, optional

Place a 12-inch (30 cm) square of dampened cheesecloth in a bowl. Squeeze juice from Seville oranges and lemons into cheesecloth-lined bowl; using spoon or grapefruit knife, scoop seeds and pulp into bowl and tightly tie cheesecloth. Strain juice.

With a sharp knife, thinly slice orange and lemon peel. Combine the peel, candied ginger with the juice in a large measuring cup. Add an equal amount of water and pour into a large, heavy-bottomed pot. Place the pulp-seed bag into pot and bring to a boil over high heat. Reduce heat; cook gently uncovered, stirring occasionally, for about 2 hours until peel is tender and mixture is reduced. If desired, cover and let stand refrigerated at this stage.

Squeeze out the liquid from the cheesecloth bag before discarding. (If the bag is too hot to handle, let it cool a little.) Measure the remaining cooked peel and liquid together and place in a clean pot. Stir in an equal amount of sugar. Bring to a rapid boil, stirring often until marmalade thickens (see Wrinkle Test, next page). Remove from heat and skim off foam. Add brandy and stir marmalade continuously for 5 minutes to ensure the rind is evenly dispersed. Ladle into hot, sterilized jars to within ¼ inch (6 mm) of top rim. Wipe jar rim and apply lids and rings until fingertip tight; do not overtighten. Process jars in a boiling water canner for 5 minutes. Let rest at room temperature until set.

Wrinkle Test
Remove marmalade from heat, place a spoonful of marmalade on a plate that has been chilled in the freezer and return it to chill for one minute. To test, push your finger into the marmalade on the chilled plate; it will form a wrinkle when the right consistency has been reached. If marmalade gel is insufficient, return mixture to a rolling boil and test again.

Tip
Savory marmalades can also be made with onions or horseradish.

Molasses Bran Muffins

Makes 12 muffins

Molasses is a by-product of sugar production. It was the most common household sweetener up until the late 19th century because refined sugar cost so much. In fact, the high cost of refined sugar was why so many recipes—old-fashioned favourites such as ginger cookies and cakes, shoofly pie, baked beans and taffy—feature molasses and are still common today. There are three types of molasses on the market: unsulphured, sulphured and blackstrap. Unsulphured molasses is the highest quality and most pure molasses. Blackstrap molasses, which should also be unsulphured, is an excellent source of iron and is high in calcium and copper. Sulphured molasses should be avoided. Molasses is produced right here in Alberta, but it is not palatable to humans. All sugar production in southern Alberta, mostly in and around Taber, hails from the sugar beet (*Beta vulgaris* subspecies *vulgaris*). Like sugar cane, sugar beets produce molasses as a by-product, but sugar beet molasses is used in animal feed, most importantly for the cattle industry.

1¼ cups (310 mL) bran cereal

1½ cups (375 mL) buttermilk

¾ cup (175 mL) molasses

½ cup (125 mL) canola or sunflower oil

1 egg, beaten

⅔ cup (150 mL) pitted dates, chopped

1¾ cups (435 mL) flour

1 Tbsp (15 mL) baking powder

1 tsp (5 mL) baking soda

pinch of salt

Preheat oven to 400° F (200° C) and spray a muffin tin with nonstick spray. Set aside.

In a bowl, mix the cereal and buttermilk and let stand for 5 minutes. Add the molasses, oil and egg, and stir to combine. Stir in the dates. Set aside.

In another bowl, sift together the dry ingredients. Fold the dry into the wet until just combined, then fill each muffin tin almost full with batter.

Bake for 12 to 15 minutes or until the tops of the muffins spring back with light pressure. Allow to cool for 5 minutes and then remove from pan.

Tip
Buttermilk and sour milk are often used interchangeably in recipes. To make your own sour milk, put 2 to 3 tsp (5 to 10 mL) of lemon juice or vinegar in a measuring cup and add enough milk for one cup of liquid. Let the mixture sit for about 10 minutes.

Sunflower Granola

A perfect start to a cold, dark winter morning, granola first became popular in the 1960s with the hippie movement. Its origins go back a bit farther, though, to Dr. John Harvey Kellogg, who in the 1870s developed the concoction as part of the Seventh Day Adventist vegetarian and whole-grain based diet at the Battle Creek Sanitarium. There is no right or wrong way to make granola, and it is suited to many ingredients. The sunflower seed featured in this granola is the only oilseed native to the northern Great Plains of North America, and it has been grown commercially in Canada since the early 1940s. Sunflower *(Helianthus annuus)* is grown domestically and commercially in Alberta. A great summer project for kids is to plant some sunflower seeds and track the growth of the plant.

4 cups (1 L) old-fashioned oats (not quick)

1 cup (250 mL) unsweet-ened, shredded coconut

1 cup (250 mL) dried fruit of choice: blueberries, cherries, sliced apricots, etc.

1 cup (250 mL) pumpkin seeds

1½ cups (375 mL) sunflower seeds

½ cup (125 mL) sesame seeds

1 cup (250 mL) wheat germ

1 cup (250 mL) chopped almonds

½ cup (125 mL) chopped cashews

⅔ cup (150 mL) maple syrup

1 tsp (5 mL) pure vanilla extract

½ tsp (2 mL) salt

¼ cup (60 mL) sunflower oil

Preheat oven to 325˚ F (160˚ C). Place all ingredients in a large bowl and mix well. Spread on a baking sheet and bake for 15 minutes. Stir and bake 10 more minutes. Stir again and bake 5 to 10 minutes more until golden brown. Cool and store in an airtight container for up to a month.

Tip
Sprinkle granola over your favourite cereal or yogurt, or simply enjoy with milk. You can also eat it plain by the handful, or you can freeze it for use at another time.

Bow Island, home of Alberta Sunflower Seeds Ltd., has a 9.1-metre (30-foot) high statue of a sunflower plant

Preserved Lemons

Although they are available all year, lemons and other citrus fruit peak during winter, and they are a welcome sunny break during our cold, snowy months. Lemons (*Citrus limon*) are a very versatile ingredient in the chef's arsenal of "secret ingredients": nine times out of ten, when something is missing from a concoction, a squeeze of lemon juice inevitably does the trick. Preserved lemons can be used in all the ways you use fresh lemon juice, yet they also offer a mysterious meatiness the juice just can't deliver. Lemons are actually a cultivated hybrid of the citron and mandarin, believed to have first been used in central India.

8 lemons, organic highly recommended

1 cup kosher salt

2 to 4 cups (500 mL to 1 L) fresh lemon juice, enough to cover the lemons

Optional Spices

2 bay leaves

4 coriander seeds

4 black peppercorns

1 cinnamon stick

2 whole cloves

Make two cuts in lemons, from the top to within ½ inch (1 cm) of the bottom, almost quartering them but not going all the way through. Pack salt into each lemon and reshape.

Place 1 tablespoon (15 mL) salt on the bottom of two 4-cup (2 x 1 L) preserving jars. Push lemons into the jars and squish them down, adding more salt and spices, if you are using, between each layer of lemon, until all the salt is used. Fill the remaining space in the jars with fresh lemon juice to approximately ¾" (2 cm) from top of jars, being sure lemons are completely covered.

Seal and store in a cool, dark part of your pantry for 4 weeks, giving the jars a little shake every once in a while. After 4 weeks, the lemons are ready to use. Remove them from the jars as needed. They can be stored in a cool, dark pantry, or in the refrigerator, if you prefer, for up to 6 months.

Variation

Try preserving a mixture of limes and lemons.

Angel Food Cake with Passion Fruit Sauce

Serves 6 to 8

Angel food cake is the quintessential "recovery from the holiday-binge" dessert! This fat-free cake is soft, airy and light. It is difficult to pin down its origin, but it likely first appeared in the late 19th century. Some people attribute angel food cake to the Pennsylvania Dutch, mainly because of their history of using special moulds to form festive cakes. Angel food cake is rare among desserts in that it is fat-free—in fact, it must be kept completely away from oils or fats (including stray bits of egg yolk) in order to achieve its characteristic spongy lightness. Before starting, is vital that all your utensils and bowls be squeaky clean.

1 cup (250 mL) sifted cake flour

1½ cups (375 mL) berry sugar, divided into two ¾-cup (175 mL) portions

¼ tsp (1 mL) sea salt

12 egg whites

1½ tsp (8 mL) vanilla or almond extract

¼ cup (60 mL) warm water

1½ tsp (8 mL) cream of tartar

Preheat oven at 375° F (190° C). Sift the flour, half of the sugar and salt, repeat 3 times and set aside. In an electric mixer, beat egg whites, vanilla or almond extract and water with cream of tartar at medium-high speed until foamy. Slowly sift in the remaining sugar, beating until you have medium-firm peaks.

Sift about ½ cup (125 mL) of the flour mixture over whites and gently fold just until flour disappears. Repeat, folding in remaining flour mixture ½ cup (125 mL) at a time. Pour batter into an ungreased 10-inch (25 cm) angel food pan. Bake until cake springs back when lightly touched, about 30 to 40 minutes. Invert pan on a cooling rack or on the neck of a bottle in order to maintain as much volume or height of the cake as possible. Cool completely and serve with passion fruit sauce.

For the passion fruit sauce, cut the fresh fruit in half and spoon out pulp. Bring the apple juice and sugar to a boil in a saucepan and cook over medium heat for about 15 minutes or until thick and syrupy. Add the passion fruit pulp and lemon juice and boil for another three minutes and remove from heat. Pour the sauce into a clean jar and refrigerate up to a week.

Passion flower (Passiflora) *grows here as an annual woody vine, but the fruit of the species is not as tasty as the tropical species that is available in Alberta grocery stores in the late fall and winter.*

Passion Fruit Sauce

1 cup (250 mL) fresh passion fruit pulp, from about 6 passion fruit

⅓ cup (75 mL) unsweetened apple juice

1 cup (250 mL) sugar

juice of ½ lemon

Bloody Caesar

Serves 1

Now known as Canada's national drink, this concoction was invented by Walter Chell in Calgary in 1969. As the head bartender at the Calgary Inn, what is now the Westin Hotel, he was asked to come up with a new drink to celebrate the opening of a new Italian restaurant on the premises. Chell experimented for three months to find the right combination and finally settled on hand-mashed clams, tomato juice, vodka, Worcestershire sauce, salt and pepper, with a celery stick for garnish. To spare bartenders and drinkers the hassle of mashing clams every time a Bloody Caesar was ordered, American entrepreneur Duffy Mott soon developed Clamato juice with Chell's assistance, and now Canadians drink about 310 million Caesars every year. Several kinds of Clamato juice are available, with different levels of spiciness to suit your palate.

1 oz (30 mL) vodka

Clamato juice, as needed

dash of Worcestershire sauce

dash of Tabasco

sea salt and pepper to taste

celery salt

1 stalk celery

Rim a tall glass with celery salt. Add vodka and fill glass with Clamato juice. Add remaining ingredients and stir, then garnish with celery stalk.

Pepper Vodka

To make your own pepper vodka to use in this recipe, simply toast ⅓ cup (75 mL) whole peppercorns in a dry pot over medium-low heat until their aroma is released, about 2 minutes. Remove from heat, and pour a bottle of good-quality clear vodka into pot. Let infuse for 1 hour, then pour back into bottle, including pepper. Keep in freezer (where all vodka should be stored).

Calgary Red Eye

A mixture very popular in southern Alberta, a Calgary Red Eye is 1 part tomato juice and 2 parts beer.

P'tit Caribou

Serves many!

Early traders in Alberta would mix the ingredients for this very alcoholic beverage together in an earthenware jug and bury it to age it. The name, "little caribou," is said to come from the red colour that reminded the hunters of caribou blood. The recipe below is a traditional version, but one modernized P'tit Caribou calls for red wine, whisky, crème de cassis and—surprise, surprise—maple syrup.

40 oz (1.18 L) white alcohol such as vodka

40 oz (1.18 L) sherry, port or red wine

Mix together and age for at least 48 hours, refrigerated.

P'tit Caribou   **Calgary Red Eye**   Bloody Caesar

INDEX

Ale, Warthog, and Cheddar Soup, 126
Apple and Quinoa Salad, 44
Apples, Caramel-dipped, 118
Artichokes, Steamed, with Lemon Butter, 106
Asparagus and Chèvre Salad, 10
Asparagus Omelette, 34
Asparagus Soup, Cream of, 16
Barley and Lentil Burgers, 58
Beef Braise, Chestnut and, 102
Beef Tenderloin, Grilled, with Sautéed Chanterelles, 54
Bison Carpaccio Salad, 94
Blueberry Ice Cream, 80
Broccoli and Tempeh Rice Bowl, 20
Brussels Sprouts, Pancetta and Pine Nut, 112
Buns, Hot Cross, 32
Burgers, Barley and Lentil, 58
Cabbage Rolls, 136
Caesar, Bloody, 158
Cake, Angel Food, with Passion Fruit Sauce, 156
Calgary Red Eye, 158
Caramel-dipped Apples, 118
Caramelized Onions and Goat Cheese Tart, 132
Carpaccio, Bison, Salad, 94
Cauliflower and Potato Gratin, 108
Cauliflower Soup, Spiced and Parsnip, 86
Chanterelles, Sautéed with Grilled Beef Tenderloin, 54
Cheddar, Soup, Warthog Ale and, 126
Cheese, Goat, Pan-crusted with Honey-drizzled Figs with, 48
Cheesecake, Ruth's Unbaked Strawberry, 38
Chestnut and Beef Braise, 102
Chicken and Mushroom Pot Pie, 90
Chowder, Potato and Roasted Garlic, 124
Cipollini and Asiago-stuffed Morels, 14
Citrus Perch, 142
Corn, Char-grilled Taber, with Jalapeño Lime Butter, 64
Couscous, 19
Cucumber and Fresh Dill Salad, 120
Currant Cooler, 76
Duck Confit with Caramelized Rutabaga and Risotto, 100
Duck, Mu Shu, with Peaches and Daikon, 56
Eggplant "Haggis", 134
Eggplant Lasagna, 60
Espresso Martini, Creamy, 116
Fennel Salad, Shaved, 42
Fiddlehead Greens, Pan-fried, 30
Steamed, Traditional, 31
Figs, Honey-drizzled, with Pan-crusted Goat Cheese, 48
Fondue, Pumpkin, 92
Frittata, Potato, 26
Fruit Smoothie, 84

Garlic, Roasted, Chowder, Potato and, 124
Gnocchi in a Sorrel Sauce, 22
Goat Cheese Tart, Caramelized Onions and, 132
Granola, Sunflower, 152
Honey Semifreddo, Bles-Wold Yogurt and, 72
Hot Cross Buns, 32
Ice Cream, Blueberry, 80
Iced Tea with Fresh Mint, 70
Jam, Onion, 68
Jerusalem Artichokes, Roasted, 110
Lamb Stock, 19
Lamb Tagine, Spring, with Preserved Lemons and Baked Olives, 18
Lasagna, Eggplant, 60
Lemongrass Vinaigrette, Mixed Citrus Salad with, 122
Lemons, Preserved, 154
Lentil Soup, Hearty, 128
Lime Butter, Jalapeño with Char-grilled Taber Corn, 64
Lobster Cocktail, 12
Maple Candied Sweet Potatoes, 114
Maple Syrup Pie, 36
Marmalade, Brandied, with Lemon and Ginger, 148
Morels, Cipollini and Asiago-stuffed, 14
Mu Shu Duck with Peaches and Daikon, 56
Muffins, Molasses Bran, 150
Mussels, White Wine and Garlic, 140
Omelette, Asparagus, 34
Onion Jam, 68
Pancetta and Pine Nut Brussels Sprouts, 112
Papardelle with Black Winter Truffles, 104
Parsnip Chips, 87
Parsnip, Spiced, and Cauliflower Soup, 86
Passion Fruit Sauce, Angel Food Cake with, 156
Pasta, Homemade, 105
Perch, Citrus, 142
Pesto, Herb, 24
Pheasant, Apple-roasted, 96
Pie Crust, Great, 75
Pie,
Maple Syrup, 36
Rhubarb, with a Meringue Crust, 40
Saskatoon, 74
Pork, Macadamia-roasted, with Maple Syrup, 98
Pot Pie, Chicken and Mushroom, 90
Potato and Roasted Garlic Chowder, 124
Potato Frittata, 26
Potato, and Cauliflower Gratin, 108
P'tit Caribou, 158
Pumpkin Fondue, 92
Pumpkin, Curried, Soup, 88

Quince, Oven-roasted, 66
Quinoa Salad, Apple and, 44
Raspberry Tart, 78
Ratatouille, Summer Squash, 62
Rhubarb Pie with a Meringue Crust, 40
Risotto, and Caramelized Rutabaga, Duck Confit with, 100
Root Vegetables, Balsamic-glazed, 146
Rutabaga, Duck Confit with Risotto and Carmelized, 100
Salad,
Apple and Quinoa, 44
Asparagus and Chèvre, 10
Bison Carpacchio, 94
Cucumber and Fresh Dill, 120
Highwood Crossing Canola, Tomato and Tempura Bocconcini, 46
Mixed Citrus, with Lemongrass Vinaigrette, 122
Shaved Fennel, 42
Spring Heirloom Tomato, 8
Salmon, Wild, en Papillote, 50
Saskatoon Pie, 74
Smoothie, Fruit, 84
Sorrel Sauce, Gnocchi in, 22
Soup,
Cream of Asparagus, 16
Curried Pumpkin, 88
Hearty Lentil, 128
Spiced Parsnip and Cauliflower, 86
Warthog Ale and Cheddar, 126
Soup. See also Chowder
Stew, Alberta, 130
Stock, Lamb, 19
Strawberry Cheesecake, Ruth's Unbaked, 38
Sunflower Granola, 152
Sweet Potatoes, Maple Candied, 114
Swiss Chard, Braised, 28
Tart,
Caramelized Onions and Goat Cheese, 132
Raspberry, 78
Tea, Iced with Fresh Mint, 70
Tempeh Rice Bowl, Broccoli and, 20
Tempura Bocconcini Salad, Highwood Crossing Canola, Tomato and, 46
Tempura, 144
Tomato and Tempura Bocconcini Salad, Highwood Crossing Canola, 46
Tomato Salad, Spring Heirloom, 8
Trout, Blackened, with Oven-dried Tomatoes, 52
Truffles, Black Winter, Papardelle with, 104
Turkey, Roasted, 138
Vodka, Pepper, 158
Yogurt with Flaxseed and Maple Syrup, 82
Yogurt, Bles-Wold, and Honey Semifreddo, 72